TRUE ADVENTURES

THE FLAG NEVER TOUCHED THE GROUND

AMERICA'S BRAVE BLACK REGIMENT IN BATTLE

HOW ONE UNIT OF SOLDIERS CHANGED THE TIDE OF WAR

© Alice Dodge

Kekla Magoon studied history at Northwestern University in the US, and loves to uncover the stories of the brave and creative people who have come before us. Her books about civil rights and social justice in America include *X*, a novel about Malcolm X co-written with his daughter, and *The Rock and the River*, about a young boy torn between his civil rights leader father and his Black Panther brother.

Kekla has been longlisted for the National Book Award, received an NAACP Image Award, and three Coretta Scott King Honors.

TRUE ADVENTURES

THE FLAG NEVER TOUCHED THE GROUND

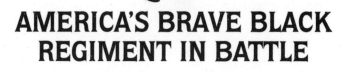

AMERICA'S BRAVE BLACK REGIMENT IN BATTLE

KEKLA MAGOON
With illustrations by Amerigo Pinelli

PUSHKIN CHILDREN'S

Pushkin Press
71–75 Shelton Street
London WC2H 9JQ

Text © Kekla Magoon 2021
Illustrations © Amerigo Pinelli 2021

First published in the UK by Pushkin Press in 2021

1 3 5 7 9 8 6 4 2

ISBN 13: 978-1-78269-305-5

Designed and typeset by Tetragon, London

Printed and bound in The United States

www.pushkinpress.com

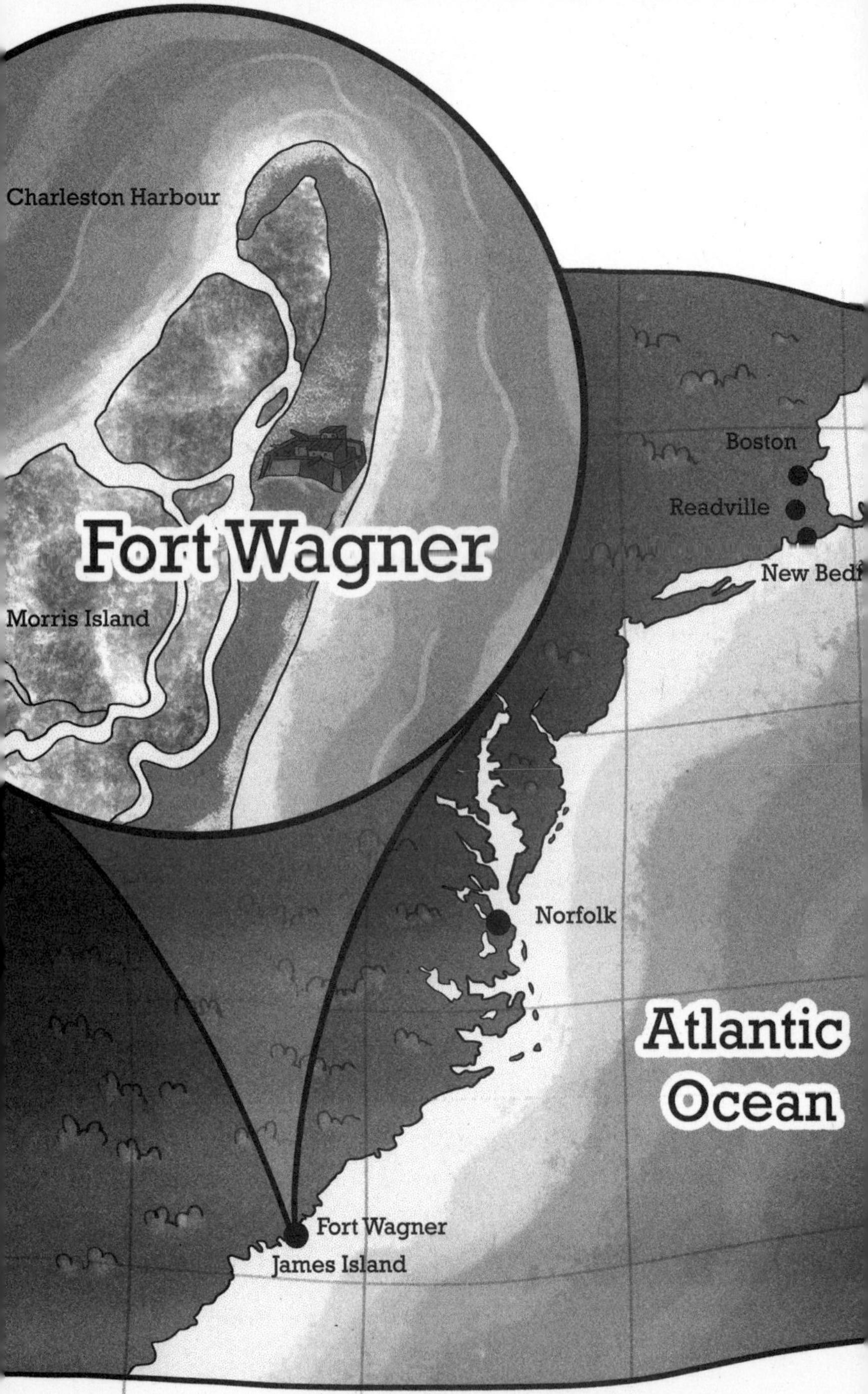

Charleston Harbour

Fort Wagner

Morris Island

Boston

Readville

New Bedf

Norfolk

Atlantic Ocean

Fort Wagner
James Island

A FRESH START

October 1859

William Harvey Carney's first breath of free air came in the form of a sneeze.

He had been lying in the warm dark, beneath a cloth in the back of the wagon, clutching his small sack of possessions to his chest. His eyes were open – vigilance was the watchword on this journey – but he had allowed himself to be lulled by the rocking rhythm of the wagon, humming the words to his favourite hymn silently in his head in time with the sway.

Suddenly the swaying stopped. William clutched his pack tighter. His heartbeat quickened. What was it? A checkpoint? A barricade? An armed band of fugitive-slave seekers? So far, he had been very lucky in his journey north, but every moment carried a heavy risk. He lay as still as he could, hoping his heartbeat wouldn't give him away. It was pounding so hard, he thought it might well be shaking the whole wagon.

He heard shuffling footsteps in the dirt. Then a deep, stretching sigh. The cloth covering him was whipped back, releasing a cloud of road dust upon him.

William sneezed.

'God bless you,' came a voice.

William squinted up into the bright morning sunshine. He already knew it was past dawn, as he had felt the sun warming the cloth for the last hour or so, but it was clearly shaping up to be a beautiful, shining day. He blinked until the face of the old-timer who owned the wagon came into focus.

'End of the line,' the old-timer said. 'New Bedford, Massachusetts.'

'What?' William said. *New Bedford*. Could it be? The words he had been dreaming about for years now had finally been uttered.

'Hop on out. You need to ride up front now.'

'Up front?' William echoed, as he scooted himself out of the wagon. His feet hit the dirt road steady.

The old-timer chuckled. 'I know you're not slow,' he said. 'I seen that book you're carrying.'

William clutched his pack tighter by impulse. The book was a notebook, into which he'd copied his favourite Bible verses. His prized possession. He had secretly gone to school back in Norfolk, Virginia, even though enslaved people weren't legally allowed to attend. The teacher, a local minister, had shown him how to read and write, and taught him the ways of God. The Christian message of service and humility appealed to him so much that he had begun studying to become a minister himself. Someday, in freedom, he might be able to have a whole Bible of his own, but for now, these copied verses were his lifeline.

He followed the old-timer along the side of the wagon. They were stopped among a copse of slim trees along the road. All was quiet, except for the shuffle of the old white man's feet, the breeze, but... William strained his ears for a moment, because there was something else – some kind of distant sound at the edge of his hearing. The sound of people, perhaps. A town.

The white man heaved himself into the driver's seat and then patted the spot beside him. 'Come along.'

'Sit right next to you?' William asked, to be sure. 'On the wagon bench?'

'Can't be riding into town with you under a blanket,' said the man. 'That'd be a mite suspicious, don'tcha think?'

'All right.' William's heart did not slow, but now it was racing for a whole new reason. He climbed up and sat as far to the side as he could, being careful not to touch the white man at all. He surely didn't want to find the limits of the old-timer's generosity.

The man nudged the reins and clicked his tongue. 'Giddyap.'

'How much further?' William asked.

'Not far. Put that bag down on the floor, between your knees. Ain't nothing gonna happen to it.'

William hesitated. The bag had been in his arms for days now. Weeks, perhaps. The journey felt endless.

The old-timer smiled. 'This is Massachusetts, boy. You gotta start acting free. 'Cause you are.'

William pressed the bag to the floorboards, securing it tight between his feet. He held his head high, and breathed in the word once again. *Free*.

The wagon rolled on, and soon they were sliding in among the hustle and bustle of the city. Houses and shops, sidewalks and squares. Horses and buggies, people scurrying, some strolling.

William took in every sight. New Bedford was everything he had dreamed of, and more. Faces in the crowd of all colours, moving together in harmony. A far cry from the strict and stilted caste system that rang clear from every angle in Norfolk.

'People come here from all over the world,' the old-timer said, 'on the ships at the wharf.' William said nothing. His own journey north had started on a boat, out of the dock at Norfolk where he and his father had worked.

His father. A little shiver crossed William's shoulders. Soon, perhaps, he'd be seeing his father for the first time in several years.

Signs in a few of the shops read 'FREE LABOUR GOODS', which the old-timer explained meant they only sold goods that had been produced without using slave labour. Several businesses they passed appeared to be Black-owned. To William, this all seemed too good to be true.

He did a double take at the sight of a white man doffing his hat to a Black woman and stepping out of her way on the sidewalk. William had never seen anything like it. The woman, who dressed in the sort of fancy clothes the lady of the plantation house had worn, nodded politely in kind. The two might have even exchanged a word of greeting. William watched in awe.

He tugged at his own worn-out work shirt, feeling less than ready to face the city, wardrobe-wise. He looked like the field hand and oyster fisherman that he was. That he had been. That was his old life in Norfolk. Here, he could start fresh.

Clothing aside, in every other way he was ready for this new adventure. More than ready. He'd been dreaming about this day for many years, ever since his father had run away to New Bedford, leaving the family behind. He had promised to make the way for William and his mother to follow, or perhaps even to buy their freedom, if he could. William's mother remained behind, waiting for the day her husband would come for her, but William hadn't wanted to wait any longer.

Freedom demanded a certain impatience, he supposed. Once you had a bug about it in your mind, it was impossible not to grasp the idea with both hands and charge forth. One thing he had learned in his studies – freedom would never be simply given. It had to be fought for. And taken.

The old-timer pulled the horse to a stop in front of a small mercantile. It had a 'free labour' sign in the window. 'Go right on in there now. Tell the owner where ya come from, and he'll getcha all set up with yer new papers.'

'Wait,' William whispered. The abolitionist had risked his life to help ferry him to freedom and… 'I don't even know your name.'

'And ya never will.' The old-timer winked and returned his attention to his work horse. 'Giddyap!' The wagon lurched forward, down the street and on into traffic.

William entered the store. The man behind the counter was tall, dark-skinned, with a thick salt-and-pepper beard. He was wrapping up purchases in brown paper for a petite Black woman.

'You have a nice day, Miss Marlene,' the shopkeeper said. As she walked towards the door, he turned to William. 'Can I help you, lad?'

William approached the counter slowly, clutching his bag. It was strange having to declare himself, after spending weeks in hiding. He took a deep breath and found his courage. Surely the Underground Railroad wouldn't lead him astray. Not this close to freedom.

'Sir, I've come on a journey,' he began. 'I was told this is a place I can trust.'

'No need to fear now, son,' the shopkeeper said. 'I know from where you come.'

William choked down his hesitation, his fear. He was in New Bedford now. Everything was new. There was no longer a threat lurking around every corner. He spoke the truth: 'I need to find my father, William Carney.'

The shopkeeper's stern face split into a broad smile. 'You've made it then, young William.'

William raised his eyebrows. 'You know my father?' His heart began racing again, this time not with anxiety and fear, but with eager anticipation.

'He's been expecting you.' The shopkeeper reached for a small notepad. 'Or hoping, at least.' He began writing an address on the top sheet.

The bell above the door jangled as a young man of about William's age came rushing in. 'They've captured John Brown!' he gushed breathlessly. 'Father, have you heard the news?' The young man carried a newspaper in his hands. He thrust it onto the desk in front of the shopkeeper.

'No,' his father responded. 'What happened?'

'John Brown?' William asked. The abolitionist was famous throughout the South for leading a raid to free slaves in Kansas Territory. Apparently, a white man who took up arms against slavery made news all over the country.

'Did you hear him speak, when he came through town last year?' The young man looked William up and down. 'No, I don't suppose you were around here back then, eh?'

'Chester, hush.' The older man turned the paper around and studied the article. 'Harpers Ferry, Virginia... attempted raid on a Federal arsenal... several killed, several captured, including Brown.'

'I attended his speech. There was this fire in his eyes!' Chester exclaimed. 'You heard him say two words, you'd be ready to take up arms and fight.' He punched the air theatrically.

'Chester, please,' his father said. 'I don't want that sort of talk around the shop.'

'Aw, Pop. There ain't no one here, 'cept...' He glanced at William.

'William,' said William. He pretended not to be as interested in Chester's storytelling as he really was. John Brown was controversial. Many people called him crazy. But escaping from slavery required courage and radical thinking. It required more than a little help from sympathetic white people – could a leader like John Brown help turn the tide?

'Chester. Get on back to work now,' said the shopkeeper. 'There are boxes in the storeroom that need unpacking.'

'But they're calling John Brown a madman,' Chester complained. 'The raid failed, but the idea… well…'

'He was an abolitionist, wasn't he?' William said casually. It was force of habit, he supposed, to pretend an outside calm when he felt something entirely different inside. He wondered if he could ever be as loud and free-sounding as someone like Chester. He could not imagine how it felt to burst into a room, to wave his arms around, drawing the centre of attention towards him.

'Not just an abolitionist. He wanted to start a war to end slavery! He was willing to die.' Chester shook his head. 'Don't know many white folks who feel that strongly.'

'There are some. Maybe more than you'd think,' the shopkeeper suggested. 'It's only a matter of time, some say.'

'Only a matter of time?' William echoed. 'What does that mean?'

The shopkeeper sighed. 'It may well mean we're going to war.'

2

REUNITED

War! The very idea stirred William to his core. He had been free for such a short time now, it all still felt new and slightly unbelievable, but there was potential in the air. A war could mean all the enslaved people in the South, like his mother, would be freed.

But William wasn't sure that would ever happen. When he thought of the white men he knew, he figured there were few who would lift a finger in defence of anything but themselves.

He walked the streets of New Bedford, admiring the storefronts and studying the people as he made his way along the map the shopkeeper had given him.

Half an hour later, William knocked at the door of a small rooming house at the outskirts of town. He had followed the shopkeeper's directions to the letter.

Moments later, a slight, dark-skinned man opened the door.

'William?' his father exclaimed. 'My God, William!' His father leaped forward and embraced him.

'Papa?' William's eyes fogged with joy and relief. He let himself be enfolded. His father smelled of salt, like he always had. The salt of sweat and the sea intermingled. Finally, something of this journey felt like home.

William had grown since last they had seen each other. He remembered his father towering over him when he was a boy. Now he was just as tall. A man in his own right. A man who had found his way to freedom.

'Come in, let me look at you,' his father said. He led William into the small wooden house, to a sitting room. 'Sit down,' his father said. 'You must be tired.'

'Yes,' William said, although he could have taken in the sight of his father in this place for hours before having any thought of closing his eyes.

The room was not especially fancy, not compared to the big houses the white families of Norfolk lived in, but it was much closer to that than to any of the slave quarters William had occupied in his life. He perched on the edge of a blue-cushioned sofa, opposite his father.

'I'm afraid I only have a few minutes before I need to leave for work,' his father said. 'You can wait for me here, and we'll get you situated.' He clapped his son's shoulder. 'And tonight, we celebrate!'

'All right,' William said. He clutched his sack of belongings. To be left alone? Here?

His father stepped out of the room for a moment, then returned. 'The woman who owns the house has gone to the market,' he said. 'You should wait in my room until I return.'

His father led William up a short flight of stairs, to a corridor with several closed doors. He opened one of the doors and showed William in. The bedroom had just the necessities – a bed, a dresser, a small table and chair, a simple rug. But the light from the large, south-facing window made the space feel warm and golden and homey.

'You must stay in here, and be very quiet until I return,' his father said, 'so as not to startle the woman of the house. It wouldn't do for her to stumble upon an unfamiliar coloured man, you hear?'

'Of course,' William agreed. There was a great comfort in this request, a respite from the hustle and bustle that characterized New Bedford. He had endured the chaos of meeting Chester, the rustle of freshly forged papers from the shopkeeper, the winding last-leg journey to his father's door, but it had all left him drained and overwhelmed. William was well accustomed to hiding quietly. To survive in slavery, it was necessary to suppress oneself constantly. Even more so on the Underground Railroad. This skill, William had in spades.

'Rest,' his father said, motioning towards the bed. 'You're home now, and thank the Lord for that.'

He closed the door behind him, leaving William alone.

William sat on the bed, his journey complete. His gaze roved the room, taking in every surface. His whole body buzzed with residual stress from his travels. He was safe now, but it was hard to really take that in. He had been on edge for so long, worried about discovery, capture, return. He paced the small room for a while. Rest? How could he rest when so much was happening, just beyond this window?

He thought about Chester's bursting energy, and how he had come and gone so freely from his father's store. Would William himself be able to do the same in the days to come? Go in and out of the boarding house at will, and explore the city? It was thrilling and terrifying to imagine.

Soon exhaustion caught up with him. He stretched out on the bed and stared at the wooden-planked ceiling. He counted the knots and cracks to try to calm his mind.

Home, whispered his brain.

Freedom, whispered his brain. *Thank the Lord for that.*

As he drifted towards the first peaceful sleep he had known in many weeks, the shopkeeper's words floated back to him. *It may well mean we're going to war. It's only a matter of time.*

Maybe. If folks decided to go to war maybe they could change everything. Maybe they—

We. William's mind perked back to consciousness long enough to ponder the pronoun. The shopkeeper had said: '*We're* going to war.'

'*We' means all of us.* William snuggled down beneath this new thought. The idea of war seemed distant, and yet… hadn't the war against slavery already begun? Abolitionists shouting from the rooftops about justice, people like John Brown taking up arms, people like the shopkeeper making free papers for folks, people like his father, brave enough to flee. People like himself. They were already fighting. What would come next?

A WHITE MAN'S WAR

Two years later – April 1861

William balanced on the rungs of the whaling ship's tallest mast, climbing carefully.

Don't look down! The conventional reminder echoed in his head as he hovered on his precarious perch. To look down was indeed dizzy-making. Instead, he preferred to look straight out.

The truth was, the risk of the climb didn't bother him. He loved being atop the mast. From this high above the harbour he could see the Massachusetts shoreline. He could see the full face of a wide, endless sea. The clean, salty air smelled of a freedom that could well be as boundless. He closed his eyes and breathed it in.

'Heave!' shouted one of his cohort from the deck below. 'Heave!'

William zipped his attention back to the task at hand. The crew on deck held ropes, tugging in unison to raise the fresh sail into place. 'A bit higher,' he called down.

When the sail arrived, William clambered among the ropes and rigging, first to the right, then to the left, securing the sail to the mast. As he shifted to the far-left side, the edge of the sail dropped a bit. Some shouting commotion had begun between the men on the deck below.

'Hey,' he called down. 'Higher on the left!' After a long moment, the sail righted itself and William finished his task.

He cast one last glance at the rooftops, the shoreline, the sea. Instead of lingering as he might have, he quickly scaled down the mast.

Worried faces among the crew greeted him when he landed. The men were clustered together around someone who had just arrived. 'What's going on?' he asked. 'What happened?'

'*It* has happened,' said one of the men. 'Shots fired at Fort Sumter, in South Carolina. The Confederate states have declared war.'

Rumblings of the possibility of a Civil War had circulated ever since a group of Southern states had seceded, or withdrawn, from the Union.

A tall man with reddish hair laid down his tools. 'Well, I suppose I'm off, then.'

'Where are you going?' asked the crew leader.

'To enlist,' said the tall man. 'If we're at war, they're going to need men to fight.'

A rumble went up among the crew. A handful of other white men laid down their tools. They began to walk away from the job.

'Not us,' said one of the Black crew members bitterly. The Union Army was open only to white soldiers. So much for the theory that the fight for freedom would need everyone to play a role. It was still a white man's world, where white men alone were granted the power to determine everyone else's fate.

'Not us,' William agreed, but his gaze stayed upon the men walking away from them. A shiver coursed through him.

That afternoon, walking home, William took a slight detour. The familiar doors of the Salem Baptist Church beckoned him. Church had always been a source of comfort to him in times of distress, and today was sure shaping up to be one of those times.

'Reverend Jackson?' he called as he entered.

The pastor was standing in the pulpit with his head bowed. 'Why, hello, William.' He stepped out of the pulpit and walked down among the pews.

'I'm sorry to interrupt,' William said. 'You've heard the news about Fort Sumter? About the war?'

Reverend Jackson shook his head sadly. 'Yes. I'm just saying a prayer for all the young men who will respond to the call.'

William felt the now-familiar blip of frustration that he could not be one of them. It had been churning in his gut since he heard the news. It was strange. He wasn't a fighter by nature, at least not like that. He had never thrown a punch, even when he'd wanted to. Especially when he'd wanted to. But still, the pain of Black freedom being entirely at the mercy of a white army struck a deep chord. So long as their fate was in white men's hands, how could they ever be truly free?

'Secession wasn't enough?' William wondered. Over the last six months, eleven Southern states had seceded, or withdrawn, from the United States of America, intending to form their own nation, called the Confederate States of America. 'They will go out of their way to draw blood over the right to hold us down?' They always had, of course. Why should now be any different?

The older white man sighed. 'The quest for power and control is inevitable, some would say.'

William nodded. It was a white man's view, suitable for this white man's landscape in which they were all trapped.

'I pray for the lives of men on both sides,' Reverend Jackson said. 'But I pray for the Union ideals to prevail.'

'Praying doesn't feel like enough,' William said.

He sank onto the front pew. There was a stirring in his belly, not unlike what he had felt back in Norfolk, the feeling that he needed to break out of this place. To become something more, something bigger than the world around him would allow. These past two years in New Bedford had shaken loose some of those old feelings of stagnation, of being trapped and suppressed… or so he had thought. Now, he found it all returning, in a way that made it hard to breathe.

The reverend sat down next to him. 'Prayer always does more than it feels like it's doing.' He clapped William on the shoulder. 'There's never been a more important time for men of faith to lead the way.'

'It doesn't feel like leading,' William answered. 'It feels like standing still.'

For all the so-called equality in the North, there were still so many things off-limits. There was still a sense of waiting. William recalled watching those white men walk off from the harbour earlier, so determined to be part of the change that was coming that they were willing to put their lives on the line for their country. It had been noble on their part, to be sure, but it had left William feeling hollow. True freedom meant choice – the choice to fight or not, the choice to stand in the light of day and declare: *This is what I believe in*.

High up on the ship's mast, he had glimpsed that kind of freedom. Now, back on earth, he realized that it had been only that – a glimpse. Brief. Revocable. Not truly his to claim at all.

'Change takes time,' Reverend Jackson continued. 'I also pray for the enslaved, for those who have yet to know freedom, that it may be swiftly delivered.'

'Do any of us yet know freedom?' William mused. 'Really know it?'

'This is a free state,' the reverend reminded him, in a sort of fatherly, I-know-best tone of voice. 'Soon, God willing, all the states will be as free.'

William stared up at the polished wooden cross above the altar. Perhaps it had been a mistake to bring his questions to Reverend Jackson. How could a white man ever understand what it felt like to be stuck in freedom's shadow?

He wished he could reach his own hand down to the South and bring people to freedom, like the workers of the Underground Railroad, or like the Union soldiers about to fight for the cause. He wished he could promise them, *Someday, you could be more than a deck hand like me*.

'Thanks, Reverend.' William stood up. 'I should get home.'

'Let us pray, before you go,' the minister said.

26

'Well, all right.' William remained standing, but he bowed his head, as he knew he was supposed to.

Reverend Jackson intoned a brief prayer, full of familiar sentiments and well-meaning thoughts. William tried to release himself to the prayer, like usual, but it was hard to focus.

What was happening? Why did he want something so different now than what he had always wanted? Why did hoping and praying suddenly feel like nowhere near enough? These two years of freedom had changed everything. God willing, more change was yet to come.

William paused on the way out the door, overcome with a feeling as strong as any he had ever felt. He might not be able to fight in this war, but he had to find a way to do something more than stand by and watch. He felt it with a certainty that shocked him, as sure as he felt God's breath on his neck when he prayed.

A CHANCE AT LAST

Two years later – February 1863

The posters must have gone up that very afternoon. They had not been there when William had left for the harbour that morning, but he saw them everywhere on his way home.

MEN OF COLOUR
54th Regiment!
*Massachusetts Volunteers
of African Descent*

$100 Bounty (at the expiration of the term of service)
Pay, $13 a month (and state aid to families)
Recruiting officer: Lieutenant J.W.M. Appleton

William stood in front of the poster for a long while. As soon as he'd seen it, he knew. He was going to enlist.

It was thrilling, to know for sure. To know so suddenly. He was going to enlist. Since the war began, he'd vaguely imagined this moment, but it all felt different now. Truly having the choice placed in front of him, being free to make it, gave his heart a jolt of pride that he could not have envisioned.

A month ago, President Abraham Lincoln had signed the Emancipation Proclamation, freeing all enslaved people in the United States. Since then, rumours had been circulating, saying that Emancipation meant other changes could be in the works. Changes like Black men finally being able to enlist – but secretly William had wondered if it would ever really happen.

'William!' called a familiar voice. Chester joined him at the shop window. 'I see you've heard the news. Today's our day!'

'Guess it is,' William answered. 'Have you told your father?'

'No. Have you?'

'Not yet.'

The friends glanced at each other in silence. William figured that Chester was likely thinking a similar thought to his own, about how his father would not understand what they were about to do.

But it didn't matter, did it? Enlisting was every man's own choice. Not his father's. They were free men. They didn't need anyone's blessing or permission to do their duty before God and country.

'We've talked about this day so many times,' Chester said. He tapped the window, and the poster, lightly with his fist. 'Hot damn.'

'Yes,' William agreed. 'Hard to believe it's really happening.'

William and Chester walked to the enlistment station. A small crowd of Black men hovered around. Some had signed already, others were waiting in line, still others were lurking undecided and trying to make up their minds. After just a few moments, William felt he could tell the difference between the three sorts of men at a glance. Those who had been the first to enlist now strode proudly among the others. They walked tall, heads high. Those still in line craned their necks eagerly to see past those in front of them. The undecideds shuffled and shook, retreated and advanced, their waffling visible.

To fight meant putting yourself on the line, to be sure, but the obvious pride that buoyed the newly enlisted men shone attractively. William wanted to feel that sense of accomplishment and power. He craned his neck. The line seemed long. How much longer would he have to wait?

Finally they made it to the front.

'You're here to enlist?' asked the white officer behind the table. He was dressed in the Union Army blue uniform. He looked sharp and capable and very much in charge. He looked strong.

'Yes, sir,' William said.

'Yes, both of us, sir,' Chester added.

'You understand that this is enlistment for military service. You are registering for the Morgan Guards, a company to be mustered into service in the Union Army.'

'Yes, sir,' Chester and William answered in unison.

'Can you write?'

'Yes, sir.'

'Fill this out, then.' The man handed them each a page to record their information. 'You will report for training at nine a.m. on March third, in front of the City Hall. Understood, soldiers?'

Soldiers.

'Yes, sir!' Chester and William echoed, loud and proud.

Soldiers.

As they moved away from the table, a younger teen pushed past them, trying to get closer to the sign-up table.

'Hey, Alex?' Chester called to him. 'What are you doing?'

'Volunteering, same as you,' the kid answered. 'They want men of colour now, don'tcha know.' He grinned as if he'd just cracked a good joke.

'A bit young to fight, aren't you?' Chester asked.

The boy raised his chest. 'Old enough to be a drummer, or to carry the flag.'

'That's madness,' said Chester. 'Last I checked you were still in Sunday school.'

'Haven't you heard, Chester, old boy? It's Monday.' Alex winked and sauntered off.

Chester laughed. 'Quite the uppity fellow. Always has been.'

William smiled too. 'Probably been spending too much time with you, then, eh?'

Chester chucked his friend in the shoulder. 'Hey, who are you calling uppity, Negro?'

They jostled each other as they made their way along.

'Well, we did it,' William said, a few minutes later, at the street corner where they would part.

'Heck, yeah,' Chester replied. 'We did it, but we still gotta… do it.'

'Yeah,' William agreed glumly. Enlisting was the easy part. Now they had to go home and tell their fathers. 'Good luck.'

'You too.'

They slapped hands and went their separate ways.

William's father paced beside the bed. 'I still don't see why you have to do this. It's not our fight.'

William gritted his teeth as he jammed his Bible and a clean shirt into his knapsack. Since the day he had enlisted, it had been the same conversation, on repeat.

'It's *all* of our fight,' William said for what felt like the hundred thousandth time. 'How can any of us truly be free if we don't stand up for freedom for all?'

His father shook his head. 'They're not gonna hand us freedom. Mark my words. We gonna be on a uphill climb for ever.'

'Maybe not,' William said. 'Maybe we can change everything. Maybe this war changes everything.' He slammed the flap of his knapsack closed, wishing it made the satisfying sort of thump of latching a trunk or slamming a door. He wanted to end this conversation, fast and firm. 'I have to go.'

'You ain't have to do nothing. You're a free man. They don't own you no more.' His father threw up his hands. 'Least they didn't up until you signed yourself away again.'

'Enlistment isn't slavery, Dad.'

His father scoffed. 'You're walking straight back into their hands, don't you see it? Down South, you're still a fugitive!'

'I'll be with the Union Army.'

'You're still a Black man. Don't you forget it. They sure won't.'

'Dad—' William wanted to keep arguing, to convince him, but there wasn't time. He picked up his pack.

'They could take you back, you know. Buy you, sell you, put you in chains! What we had in Norfolk wasn't the worst of it. You don't know what you're risking.'

'Dad—'

'You got this idea in your head about being a soldier. You're smart. You care. That's all good.' His father put his hands on William's shoulders. 'But you're too soft for war.'

The comment cut William to the quick. His worst fear, voiced by the man he most wanted in his corner. He shrugged away. 'I wasn't too soft for the Underground Railroad,' he retorted. 'I know how to work, how to fight.'

'All this time, talking like a man of God. Now you're gonna go out killing?' His father's voice cracked. Suddenly William saw through all the anger, all the arguments. His father was simply afraid. And that was not what he needed today, on the day he had to be braver than he'd ever been.

'I'm leaving now,' William said, his own voice thickened with emotion. 'Can we just say goodbye and pretend as if you support what I'm doing?'

The two stood in silence for a moment. William smoothed his clothes and swallowed the knot in his throat. He didn't know how else to explain the sense of calling he felt. He was risking everything in this service, that much was true. His life, his freedom. But the truth of his father's words did not make them any less hurtful.

'Very well,' his father said. 'I know you'll make me proud.'

The words William had wanted to hear meant somewhat less when he had to beg for them. He shouldered his pack and tossed one last glance at his father. They may not have agreed about the war in that moment, but William was determined to make sure that his service would make his father proud, for real.

It had to.

5

TOO SOFT FOR WAR?

William searched for familiar faces in the crowd of over a hundred soldiers reporting for duty. Many of the men were taller than his own five foot eight. They seemed older, more confident. William felt small all of a sudden. A trill of anxiety whispered through him. What if his father was right? What if he didn't really have what it took?

He struggled to shake off the doubt, newly fomented by his father's final words: *You're too soft for war.* Why couldn't Dad have found something more positive to say? A bold whisper William could carry with him through the difficult days to come, rather than these seeds of doubt.

A sergeant called roll and men stepped forward one by one to receive their supplies.

'Carney, William.'

'Present.' William pushed through to the front. The sergeant checked his name off a list. A man standing beside the table reached into a crate and pulled out a pair of knitted woollen mittens. He handed them to William. They were thick and warm. 'Thank you,' William said.

'Stand in formation,' the soldier said, nodding to the right-hand side of the crowd, where the men were standing in loose rows.

William stood with the others as the sergeant made his way through the list.

'Perkins, Chester.'

William lifted his head when his friend's name was called. He waved as Chester received his mittens and joined the formation.

'Are you nervous?' William whispered, once Chester was beside him.

'Nah,' Chester answered. 'It's gonna be amazing.'

His friend was smiling, but William noticed that he was clutching the new mittens hard against his chest, and softly stroking their thumbs.

'Me neither,' he lied.

When roll call was complete, the Morgan Guards packed up to travel from New Bedford towards the city of Boston. They stopped in Readville, on the outskirts of the city, at a place called Camp Meigs, where they'd have their basic training.

William and Chester, along with the rest of the company, strode eagerly into camp and looked around. The wide clearing was punctuated by the occasional copse of sparse trees. A few wooden buildings stood at one edge, while the opposite side was punctuated by a series of campfires.

Smoke from the wood fires rose above pits a few yards from the start of the woods. The smell of roasting meat wafted to them. William's stomach spoke in response to the mouth-watering aroma. It had been a tiring trip.

'Wow,' Chester said, studying the surroundings as earnestly as William. The camp seemed run-down, the buildings sagging and worn. They appeared no worse than the slave quarters William had known, but little better.

This place would be their new temporary home.

'Company, atten-tion!'

The troops scrambled to stand in loose rows. William pulled his chest up proudly, fists pressed against the sides of his thighs. It was what the other men were doing. He had seen soldiers standing at attention before.

Several officers, all white men, strode out of one of the wooden buildings. They crossed the field towards the new arrivals, and mounted a small elevated wooden platform to address the troops.

'Welcome to Camp Meigs,' the officer in charge said. 'My name is Captain Willard. You men of the

Morgan Guards will training to be Company C, the 54th Massachusetts division.'

Captain Willard stood with his hands clasped behind his back. His posture seemed both regal and calm at once. 'This unit will be the first of its kind raised in the North.' He paused. 'Now, plenty of people don't think a coloured unit will work.'

A restless murmur rose up from the men.

Captain Willard nodded. 'Yes, you've heard it, I know. Those of us here' – he waved a hand at the officers beside him – 'took this unit as volunteers. We know you men will do us proud.'

A cheer went up.

'Line up over here for your tent assignments,' the captain announced.

Once they saw how the process was going, Chester and William clustered together in hope of being assigned to the same tent. Chester kept count of the men before them, and the pair jostled about, trying to stay amid a small pack of five or six.

'You five,' the quartermaster said, when they got to the front.

'Yes,' Chester said beneath his breath, when the group included them both.

The quartermaster handed each man a small bedroll.

'Hi, I'm Ephraim,' said a scrappy lad about their age.

'William.'

'Chester.'

'Pleased to meet you. Pleased to be here! Isn't it something?' Ephraim chattered.

The three shook hands and walked towards their assigned tent. Their other tent mates were Marvin and Clem, who seemed a few years older. The two of them settled near each other at the back of the tent, while the three younger men clustered at the front. Not like there was much space between the front and back of the tent, and everything was amicable, but it quickly felt like social lines had been drawn.

Like Chester, Ephraim was a cheerful, chatty sort. The pair hit it off quite quickly, and William listened and smiled along with their banter. They spread out their bedrolls and tucked away their packs, settling into the unfamiliar space. Soon, William supposed, it would be familiar, but at the moment it was a warm, dim space full of near strangers.

Voices and rustling footsteps arose outside. Suddenly their tent flap was thrown back. 'Men of C Company, report,' a voice said from beyond.

The five soldiers scrambled out of the tent and hustled to stand at attention on the dry grass. A few other tent groups hurried to get in order as well. A Black man in uniform stood waiting for them.

'My name is Sergeant Major Lewis Douglass,' he said. 'Put down your things and come get your food.

Training begins first thing in the morning.' Then he turned and strode to the next group of tents.

'Wow,' Chester breathed. 'That's Frederick Douglass's son!'

'Really?' William asked, craning his neck to get a better look. Frederick Douglass, born into slavery in the South himself, had escaped and become a famous leader of the abolitionist movement. 'How do you know?'

'I've seen him in New Bedford,' Chester answered. 'When his father came to speak.'

William gazed after Sergeant Major Douglass with pride. If his own father, who worshipped Frederick Douglass's every word, could see him now, he'd know William was on the right side. William made a note in his mind to write this news to his father at the first chance he got. In fact, he planned to write home often, to tell of his courage and commitment. That would show his father what he was really made of.

'I thought all the officers would be white,' William said.

Ephraim nodded. 'They are, but some of our enlisted have been appointed to leadership ranks.'

'Frederick Douglass's son, for sure,' Clem added. 'They put smart guys like that in charge.'

The soldiers headed towards the cook fires, where cauldrons of simmering stew awaited them. One by one, they held out their tin bowls for a scoop of the good stuff. A cook plopped a chunk of bread on each dish too. They gathered on the grassy field to dig in.

'Mmm,' Chester moaned. 'Army food is good.'

'Camp food is good,' Ephraim corrected. 'I hear it's different once we're on the move.'

'When will that be?' Alex asked, the young teen coming over and squatting down to join them. He had been right – he hadn't been too young to enlist as a drummer boy.

'Hey, kid,' William said. It was nice to see a marginally familiar face. They had just arrived at camp, which was an adjustment in itself. The thought of moving out, moving towards battle, set butterflies in his stomach. By the time it happened, they would be ready, he told himself. By then, he would know what to expect and how to handle himself.

'I don't know when,' Ephraim answered Alex. 'When we're trained, I guess?'

'When will that be?' Alex repeated, with a mouthful of bread.

'Oh, for—' Chester slugged Alex in the shoulder, causing his eyes to go wide and his cheeks to work double-time to keep him from swallowing too early. The others laughed.

The boys chattered on among themselves, imagining the adventures they were about to embark on. They spun tales of marching onto an open field, facing a similar row of Confederates. They made explosion sounds and flared out their hands, simulating cannon shot bursting like fireworks around them. They imagined leaping forward into a line of Rebs, bayonets affixed, and slaying man after man. They laughed, and took turns proclaiming themselves the bravest.

William sat quietly and looked around. The last time he'd been surrounded by a group of all-Black men like this was back in Norfolk, and never this many at once. It was something, the idea that they could group up like this and have the chance to fight. The yarns they spun sounded both exciting – and vicious. William sliced his hunks of meat and potatoes into bite-sized pieces, listening. Talk of rifles and bayonets made a good story, but as he listened, he found himself gazing at the short, sharp pocketknife in his hand and imagining it wielded against human flesh.

You're too soft for war.

William took the handle of his pocketknife in his fist and slammed the blade down hard into the heart of a firm carrot. Damn it. Barely one night in, and he was already having second thoughts about what being in the army would entail? That could not stand.

'I've got one,' he said, chiming into the conversation for the first time. 'In the revolution, you know, they used to say to the soldiers, "Don't fire until you see the whites of their eyes."'

'Yeah?' Alex leaned forward. 'That's the way you do it?'

William had no idea. 'Oh yes,' he said, regardless. He pantomimed holding a rifle. 'Picture a forest battle. Not an open field. You wait behind a tree, or a rock – something big like that – while their line approaches. They don't know you're there. You stand silent.' He paused.

'Yeah?' Alex breathed. He took up a rifle-bearing pose, echoing William's.

'Shh.' William took his hand off his mock rifle and put a finger to his lips, then put it back. 'Wait for it. Wait for it. Watch them approach. You can see three of them from where you're hiding. Pick a man. One of the three. Let them come closer. Closer…'

Alex's hands tightened around his fake rifle. 'Wait till you see the whites of his eyes?'

'That's right,' William said. 'Closer. Just a bit closer. Ready… aim…' He paused again. He knew he was delaying the inevitable, but something held him back. The group stared at him, caught up in the suspense he had created. They were waiting.

Ever impatient, Alex picked up the tale. 'And then, BLAM!' He pantomimed popping out from behind the tree to make the shot.

The others cheered.

'That was a good one.' Alex grinned in the firelight. 'This is gonna be awesome.'

'Awesome,' William echoed, though the imagining had left him slightly queasy. Tonight it was just an exciting story, and one he couldn't even bring himself to finish. Tomorrow, or someday soon, it could be real. He could be looking in the eyes of a man – a fellow human man – and have to take that shot. A chill passed over him.

Why hadn't he been able to finish the story? It didn't mean he was soft, he told himself. Valuing human life, valuing all of God's creation, was not soft. Having compassion didn't mean he didn't have what it took to fight in this war. Did it?

Across the yard a wagon pulled in carrying a large load. A handful of soldiers were called over to meet the arrival. They pulled back the tarp and began unloading rifles from a large stack. The whole group of men fell quiet for a moment as they turned to watch.

William swallowed hard. It was getting more real by the moment.

'Hoo-ee!' Chester whooped. 'It's about to be our time.'

A RIFLE IN HIS HANDS

First thing in the morning, bugle calls echoed. William stepped out of the tent into a chilly misty pre-dawn. The bugle's warble continued, joined by drums. Alex, now in the music corps, marched happily alongside the bugler, pounding at the skin of the drum. Beside him, another young man marched, holding a long stick upright in his hands. The colour guard, William supposed, practising formation with the rest of them, although there was not yet a flag to be held.

'Load up your packs,' Sergeant Major Douglass called. 'Training means carrying what you'd carry in the field.'

William and the others loaded up their packs and shouldered them. They filled their canteens with water and strapped them over their shoulders.

They each had a belt where ammunition could be kept – although they hadn't been given any yet – and a food pouch loaded with hardtack biscuits and a bit of salt pork.

They hurried down to the parade ground, in front of the officers' quarters.

'Company, atten-tion!'

William pulled his shoulders back and stood with his fists firmly at his sides as he had been taught.

Officers came through the ranks, nudging the men into straight lines. 'You're to be addressed by the colonel,' the officers informed them. 'Look sharp!'

William was certain he had never looked sharper in his life, all suited up and soon to become a real Union soldier.

'Atten-tion!' The voice came from an average-tall white man with a curved-down moustache and a scrap of beard beneath his lower lip.

'My name is Colonel Robert Shaw. I am the commanding officer of the 54th regiment. You men will be a fine regiment. Of this, I am sure. Now, your captains will see to your training. Put your hearts into it, and soon you'll be ready to take the field.'

William stood proudly in the ranks, shoulder to shoulder with his fellow soldiers.

'Report to the supply shed for your training weapons,' Colonel Shaw concluded. 'Dismissed!'

William waited in the pleasant early spring air, chatting with others while the sergeants handed out rifles.

'Here you go, Carney.'

A rifle was handed to him. William grasped it with both hands. His rifle. William had never even held a gun, and now he had one of his very own.

He took in every inch of the long metal barrel and smooth wooden handle. The trigger mechanism gleamed. As a piece of machinery, it awed him. It was impossible to touch and hold it without reverence for its power. It was equally impossible to forget the cruel and life-taking nature of that power.

'Can you believe it?' Chester crowed. He took the rifle to his shoulder and pointed it towards the trees.

'Men, fall in!' called the rifle instructor. William listened closely as the man explained the rifle loading procedure. It sounded complicated in a way that seemed exciting, challenging and fun. They all tried it together, slowly.

'Shoulder arms!' the instructor began. William held the rifle vertically at his side, leaning it against his right shoulder and cupping the base with his right hand. His left hand remained at his side.

'Load!' shouted the instructor. William reached across and took his rifle from his shoulder, bringing it down to plant the base on the ground between his feet. He reached his hand back into his cartridge pouch, pretending there were ammunition rounds waiting.

'Handle cartridge!' William pantomimed pulling out a two-inch-long paper-wrapped cylinder, which would contain gunpowder and a Minié-ball bullet. He tried not to think about the bullet, but focus on the process.

'Tear cartridge!' William brought his hand to his mouth. The way to open the paper cartridge was to pinch a corner with your teeth, tear the tip away, and spit it out, while holding the paper tube tightly.

'Drop cartridge!' William poured imaginary gunpowder into the mouth of the rifle, pressed the paper tube and bullet down after it. *Focus on the process*, he reminded himself. *The rhythm*. It was soothing, in a way. It forced his mind to zoom in and focus, to shut out the world, to shut out his thoughts.

'Draw rammer!' The rammer was a metal rod held in a narrow tube alongside the gun barrel. This part, William got to do for real. He grabbed the wider top of it, called the tulip, between his fingers and pulled up until the rammer came free of its housing. When it was loose, he turned it over so the tulip faced down. He poised it delicately into the mouth of the gun, holding it at a forty-five-degree angle against the top of the bullet.

'Ram cartridge!' William pressed the rammer down deep into the rifle barrel. Had there been a real bullet and powder inside, it would have been pressed neatly and firmly down to the base of the weapon, ready to fire. *Process. Rhythm.*

'Replace rammer!' This part was important, William knew. The rifle would cease to be usable if he ever lost his rammer, or if he accidentally fired too soon – with the rammer still inside. He pulled the rammer back out of the barrel and slid it back into its holding tube. The instructor drilled them repeatedly about the return of the rammer. William swore to himself that he'd never forget.

'Prime!' William eased the rifle up at his side, resting the back on his cartridge pouch, holding the barrel at about eye-level, pointing forward at an angle. He reached into a second pouch on his belt and removed a firing cap, pulling back the hammer and pressing it onto the cone of the rifle.

'Shoulder arms!' Back to vertical position, against his shoulder, with the rifle now ready to fire.

'Ready! Aim! Fire!' shouted the instructor to finish the drill. William lifted the gun horizontally, looked along the barrel, aimed at an imagined target in the distance and pulled the trigger. *The whites of their eyes*, echoed the voice inside his head.

With no real powder inside, the trigger merely clicked. Still, William felt a sense of accomplishment rattling up alongside the uneasy feeling that lingered.

All this time, talking like a man of God. Now you're gonna go out killing? His father's words floated back to him.

'Good!' the instructor shouted. 'Again. Load!'

They repeated the drill over and over. The goal was to get faster and faster at loading. To have it feel like second nature. The best soldiers, the instructor told them, could do the full load in fifteen seconds.

Soon the rhythm of it became entirely lulling. William found it hypnotic, the balance between the simplicity and the challenge of being so precise. It was easy to forget, briefly, in the excitement of a loading drill, that their ultimate targets would be men. It was a relief to let himself forget.

'Shoulder arms!' shouted the instructor. 'Make ready, take aim, fire!'

It was the word 'aim' that did it, every time. William imagined staring down the barrel into another man's eyes, and the reality came back, fierce and firm. They were practising how to kill, maim, put down the enemy.

But the enemy was still a man.

'When do we get to fire for real?' Ephraim asked.

'We don't expend real bullets in training,' the instructor explained. 'But you'll practise the process over and over so you'll be ready when the time comes.'

When they weren't drilling with rifles, they marched. They marched in formation for hours every day. The marches were long and gruelling. They walked until their feet ached, until blisters formed and bled and had to be wrapped. Then they walked some more, until the blisters scabbed over and their feet were as tough as field hands'.

Then they drilled some more, practising following commands, moving as a unit, firing and firing and firing.

When they were not training, they rotated through various chore teams: cooking, cleaning, caring for the officers' horses, organizing supplies. Collectively, the men took care with their surroundings. William was on cleaning duty one day, sweeping out the officers' mess, when he overheard the officers say, 'These coloured boys keep this place cleaner than any regiment I've ever seen.'

William smiled and shook his head. White men were always thinking things like that: expecting the worst, surprised when Black people ended up doing the best. Those white officers didn't know what it meant to the Black troops to be here. They couldn't imagine.

'Guess we always shoulda had 'em cleaning up after us,' another officer replied. 'Who says coloureds can't be good for the war effort?' The two left, laughing.

William's smile faded. He gripped the broomstick harder than ever. He vowed that the sweeping job he was about to finish would be his best ever. These were the same officers that trained them, that encouraged them, that kept saying the 54th regiment would show the world what coloured troops were capable of. Was it all for show? Were they joking when they said they knew coloured soldiers' potential? Did they all secretly believe Black troops were only good for cooking and cleaning?

You're too soft for war. Suddenly his father's words meant something different to William. He saw it all in a fresh light. A new understanding of the constant cruelty he had known at the hands of white men crystallized. Soft? He wasn't soft. He just... valued humanity. As God intended. In the white world, that was a weakness. You had to be willing to maim, kill, enslave, destroy to get what you wanted. To get ahead. To make and keep yourself free.

At supper time, the commanding officer addressed the troops, repeating the now-familiar sentiments about their promise, about his confidence in them. William normally felt pride in these words, but tonight they rang hollow. In his heart, he recommitted himself to the cause – not the white men's cause, but his own. He was here as a free man, fighting for the freedom of other men, that they would not be subject to cruelty any longer.

Absolutely, William would fight. And when the time came, yes, he would shoot and even kill. Not because he didn't care, but because he cared so deeply. America had made promises of freedom that it was currently failing to keep. That was the fight, and it was well worth his sacrifice.

'Get some rest, and in the morning, pack up your tents,' Colonel Shaw said. 'Training is over.'

Excitement buzzed through the ranks. The moment they had been waiting for was upon them, finally.

That night, William, Chester and Ephraim gathered around the small campfire with several other men. They sang along with the familiar songs and listened to a few unfamiliar ones. The hopeful, stirring mood of the men was noticeable.

'They underestimate us,' William said, to no one in particular.

'What?' Chester said, glancing over at his friend, with his trademark eagerness in his smile.

William shook his head. The last thing he wanted to do was bring anybody down. 'Never mind,' he said. 'I was thinking out loud.'

'Yeah?' Chester said. 'About tomorrow?'

'Yeah,' William answered. *And the day after that. And as long as it takes to show them who we are.*

THE STARS AND STRIPES

18th May 1863

Boston was the greatest place William had ever laid eyes on. New Bedford was a city, to be sure, but it was nothing compared to the hustle and bustle and tangled streets of Boston. A thrill rippled through him at the feeling of being but one small speck on the face of the city. It was a similar feeling, if strangely opposite, to how he felt looking out over the open sea — a sense of possibility and opportunity, a sense of a whole world to be explored and someday having the chance to do it.

Today, it felt like Boston was all decked out to welcome him. Hundreds, maybe thousands, of people lined the streets. The crowds waved and cheered.

'Golly,' Chester whispered. 'Look at them all.'

'They're here for us,' William answered. He pulled his shoulders back, pressing his chest forward proudly. 'To see it with their own eyes. We are making history.'

Such a sight had never been seen before anywhere in the United States – Black men marching in formation, dressed in uniforms of military blue. A thousand men, marching to meet the Stars and Stripes, marching to represent the nation. William had never felt so tall.

The 54th regiment marched in parade formation through the streets of Boston. William wondered when the crowds would fade, but they didn't. Onlookers leaned over balconies and waved from stoops and storefronts. When they arrived at the Boston Common, a spacious park in the centre of town, it was full of waving flags and a stage draped in decorative bunting.

The soldiers filed into their ranks before the stage. Up above, Governor John Andrew of Massachusetts stood waiting, alongside the famed Frederick Douglass and a handful of other prominent men. Colonel Shaw climbed up beside them. The men shook hands.

The ceremony was important, William knew. It was the Governor and the Commonwealth of Massachusetts officially drawing them into service as part of the Union Army. When Frederick Douglass stepped to the podium, William paid closer attention. He had read the abolitionist's writings for many years, but to see him in person was quite something else. He was a tall man, with a broad face, a beard, and hair that winged out gloriously from the sides of his head. He held himself upright, like a man with nothing pressing him down, a man who would not bow.

Listening to the great man, William vowed he would not bow either.

Near the end of the ceremony, the governor stepped forward and invited Colonel Shaw to join him near the podium.

'This occasion is a novel and peculiar one,' Governor Andrew began. 'Today we recognize the right of every man in this Commonwealth to be a *man* and a citizen.'

Freedom, William thought. He had craved it since he was a child, and now he had it, but so many others still toiled, enslaved. William thought back to his life in Norfolk, Virginia, feeling grateful that his parents had taught him the importance of freedom. How many others hovered in hope throughout the South?

Governor Andrew continued, 'I now have the honour, on behalf of the coloured ladies of Boston, to present you with the American Flag for the 54th regiment of Massachusetts volunteers. Before it shall ever be surrendered to the foes may its white stripes be spattered with the red blood of those who bear it in the field.'

Spattered with the red blood… A slight chill passed over William's shoulders. Soon, he would see such a battlefield. His breath quickened as his mind warred between emotions: excitement… determination… anticipation… fear.

No. He wasn't afraid. He couldn't be afraid. He was a free man, doing what was right. God was on his side too, he was sure of it. How could he fear?

The crowds cheered. The soldiers around him stood at full attention. William worked hard to remain as stock-still and proud as they all seemed. To be one of this number was the greatest honour of his life.

Governor Andrew brought forth a second flag, this one bearing the arms of the State of Massachusetts. 'This banner has never been surrendered to the foe. Hold onto the staff, if every thread is blown away, your glory will be the same.'

Colonel Shaw accepted the flags with a stately nod. 'I will strive to faithfully perform all that is possible for the glory of the 54th regiment volunteers.' He looked out over the brown faces of his troops. 'I consider it an honour to lead men who exhibit such unmistakeable evidences of patriotism.'

William shivered with anticipation. It was excitement, he reassured himself. Not nervousness.

Not fear. The tremors rippling through him were tremors of pride and honour. He gazed up at the Union flag, its thirty-four proud stars shining in the sunlight.

As goes the flag, so go the soldiers, the officers liked to say.

They were going to war.

8

ON THE THRESHOLD OF HISTORY

28th May 1863

As always, the sea smelled of freedom.
Perhaps more so today than ever, William
thought, in his uniform with his rifle at his
shoulder and his regiment surrounding him. How
many people – coloured men especially – had stood
so clearly on the threshold of history? Today, the
54th regiment did. The governor's words still radiated
through him, filling him with feelings of pride and
nobility.

William, Chester and Ephraim gathered round
with the others, waiting to board the steamer.

'Never been on a boat,' Ephraim said. 'Can't say
I'm looking forward to it.' He gazed at the huge ship
with trepidation.

'Won't be so bad,' Chester said. 'Just a way to get from one place to another, eh?' But he shuffled from one foot to the other, like he did when he was nervous.

The ship's name was painted on its side: *DeMolay*. They stepped onto the deck and William met the familiar sway of wood beams buoyed by water.

'Oh,' Ephraim moaned. 'Nope. Do not like it.'

As the whole regiment loaded, Ephraim's sentiment seemed increasingly popular. The soldiers crowded the ship and settled in for the long ride. Many already seemed unsettled by the ship's sloshing wake. If they didn't like this, the discomfort would only get stronger as they went out to sea, William knew.

'Last time our people were carried on great ships, it didn't end well,' Chester said, his cheeks slightly purple. 'Can't you feel that? I swear, I can feel it.'

William couldn't. But he was used to the water, after all those years working in the harbour. It felt good to him, the slight lulling. This ship was large enough that the waves would not easily overtake it or shake it.

'Just a way to get from one place to another,' he reminded Chester and Ephraim. 'It won't be so very long, not for us.'

Back on the dock, at the front of the now-dispersing crowd, the great bearded orator waved goodbye. Frederick Douglass was no doubt waving to his son, William supposed, but he raised his hand

and waved back anyway. Maybe, just maybe, the great liberator was blessing them all.

3rd June 1863

The 54th regiment disembarked from the *DeMolay* steamer. A sign at the harbour said 'BEAUFORT, SOUTH CAROLINA'.

'Whew,' Chester said. 'So much for springtime.'

Indeed, the South Carolina air was muggy and warm. It felt like summer had arrived a bit early. As compared to the cool sea breeze, it was stifling.

Chester and Ephraim, like many of the men, were glad to be on solid ground again. They shouldered their packs and their rifles and marched along with the unit. Even to William, it felt good to stretch his legs and feel the world wide-open again. They marched in formation through the town, much as they had done in Boston.

And as in Boston, they walked with pride, as more and more spectators came to witness the Black soldiers. White people and Black people alike crowded along sidewalks, in yards, against fences, to see the Union Army.

On the whole, the people were quieter. There was not the roar of crowds screaming and cheering them on. This was a different kind of scrutiny. Some of the white people didn't like what they were seeing, but for the enslaved, it was a different story. William noticed Black face after Black face looking on in awe, realizing that these men who looked like them had come in arms to free their people. What a wondrous sight it must have been!

William pulled his shoulders back, walking tall and proud. This, this was what it was all about. This was why they had come.

By the time the regiment settled into camp that evening, William felt completely energized, and exhausted. His brain buzzed with everything he had seen, from the grateful enslaved people soon to be freed, to the new and sultry landscape of this unfamiliar coast. The trees were different, even from those most common to his first home in Virginia. Their moss-draped shadows leered eerily in the dusk.

His skin tingled with the knowledge that they were no longer safe in Massachusetts, in training, although the basic make-up of the camp they had made echoed what they had before. They were in foreign territory, at least as far as the Confederacy was concerned. It felt strange to be in the United States but not in the United States at the same time.

The feeling in camp was different now. Guards and sentries were posted day and night to keep watch for intruders and spies. The trees surrounding them here felt less like a shield or a protection, and more like an enclosing darkness from which any threat could emerge.

William settled around the small fire with his friends, listening to Ephraim and Chester's banter. He pulled out a small square of paper, leaned towards the firelight and began writing to his father about their arrival. He would make it sound exciting. Transformative. He would shut out all thoughts of the nighttime and remember how it had felt to be in the light.

10th June 1863

'One, two, three, heave!' William strained along with ten other men to lift the fallen tree. They scuttled fifty yards to the left and set it down near the pile of others. William wiped his forehead as they strode back to get the next one. Building a campsite from scratch in the wilderness was no small task. Suddenly he appreciated the previous clearing significantly more than he had.

'Men, muster!' shouted the captains, interrupting their clearing work. The soldiers bustled to arms and rushed into formation. *This is it*, William thought. *Our time to fight*.

The men shouldered together, eager for their orders.

'We are being called to serve. Be ready to move out.'

Yes. William thought through the familiar firing procedure. *Load. Retrieve cartridge*.

'Company C, Company F, hold fast,' the commander said.

No.

'What?' Ephraim whispered.

'I don't know,' William answered. They stood with the rest of their company as the others moved out.

As the camp emptied, their captain strode in front of them. 'We are to remain behind and guard the camp,' he informed them. The men stood respectful and quiet, though William was sure they all groaned inside, as he did. Finally, the 54th's moment had come, and they were left behind to safeguard a bunch of tents?

The officers rapidly pointed out the soldiers' assignments and put them on a rotation.

'The camp is important,' William reminded Ephraim as they walked to their sentry posts.

Ephraim kicked the dirt. 'Yeah, sure.' He rolled his eyes. 'This is our big moment to shine.'

Inside, of course, William felt like Ephraim did. Now they were the sentries, guarding camp while others went to battle. He tried to shake off the feeling. It was all right. Someone had to stay behind. It was OK.

This, too, is war, William reminded himself. But it felt disappointing nonetheless. When would he have his chance to prove himself?

9

A BROKEN PROMISE

'Totally unfair,' Chester grumbled. 'One call to action, and we don't even get to go.'

'It doesn't seem like that much happened,' William answered.

'Still,' Chester said. 'We haven't even been out of camp!'

'Except to *move* camp,' William said. 'Seems like they can't decide where to put us.'

'What if they never use us?' Chester complained. 'You know how they talk. They think we're good for nothing, and the higher-ups think it even more so.'

William nodded. He had heard the officers say as much. And some of the older men in camp said they thought this whole coloured-unit idea was just a way for the Union Army to keep looking good to Northerners. What if they were right?

'Hey,' Chester called out to Alex, the drummer boy, who was crossing the campground along with a few others from the musician corps and colour guard. They had gotten to go to Darien along with the rest of the regiment. 'What was it like out there?' Chester asked.

Alex and his friends came over. William recognized the tallest one as the bugler, Aaron, and a stockier, dark-skinned lad as John Wall, the colour guard – the boy who carried the unit flag.

'Strange,' said the colour guard. 'It wasn't much of a fight. No one knows why they thought they needed us.'

'Things were quiet until the commander, Colonel Montgomery, ordered a whole town burned!' the tall boy exclaimed.

'A whole town?' Chester echoed.

The boys nodded. 'Houses, stables, general store. Basically anything with walls. Whoosh!' The tall boy pantomimed things going up in flames.

'People were fleeing. Women, children,' said John Wall.

'Why?' William asked. It seemed like a strange choice. 'Was there a threat?'

'We don't know,' said Alex. 'But our guys had to do some of it. Always have to follow orders.' He shrugged. 'Guess the officers had their reasons.'

'Where was Colonel Shaw?' Chester asked.

'He didn't seem too happy about it,' John Wall said. 'Guess Montgomery outranks him?' The boys wandered back towards their tents.

William stared after them, horrified. What reason could there be for burning a town, for sending people scattering in fear, rendering them suddenly homeless? After all the training, it seemed like second nature to follow orders from the officers, but the orders had always made sense. How strange it must have felt to have to do something so unexpected. So cruel.

Their training was about coming to terms with the possibility of shooting and killing a man or striking him with a bayonet. William knew that. He was preparing himself for it. That was war. But... burning a town? Displacing women and children? Where was the line between righteous battle in good faith, and unconscionable destruction?

The quest for power and control is inevitable, some would say. The white officers' highest aims were not always noble, it seemed. William's stomach roiled with this knowledge. No doubt they'd soon face yet another test of their leaders.

Just then, Ephraim scampered across the campground towards them. 'Pay day!' he shouted. 'Come and get it!'

Chester and William caught up with him. They had wondered when they might see their next pay. It was supposed to come every month, but apparently nothing worked quite as it was supposed to when there was a war on.

The three friends crowded into the growing line to get their money.

'Carney,' William said, when his turn rolled around.

The paymaster checked his name off a list and handed him money. 'That's seven dollars per month. Next!'

William hesitated. Behind him, Chester crowded closer, eager for his turn. William held him back with an elbow. He wanted to understand. 'Seven? But… it's supposed to be thirteen.'

The paymaster sighed. 'Coloured infantry now get ten dollars a month, minus three for your clothing fee. Next!' He rattled off the answer as if he'd answered this a hundred times. He probably had.

'But—' William protested. He had seen the recruitment poster with his own eyes. Thirteen dollars a month was the amount the Union Army had promised.

'Move along!' The paymaster's guard pushed William out of the way.

'This is some bull crap,' Chester declared moments later, staring at his own wanting handful of pay. 'They lied to us!'

'Not a lie,' Sergeant Major Douglass corrected, coming up beside them. 'A broken promise. We signed an agreement with specific terms, and they are bound by it.'

'Yeah!' Chester exclaimed. 'They can't get away with this.'

William wasn't so sure. It might be wrong, but he'd seen powerful white men do pretty much anything they wanted to Black men, no matter what they had promised. It would be a hundred, a thousand times worse to imagine what the government or the army could do to a handful of Black soldiers. Perhaps they should be grateful they'd been paid at all.

'Men, gather round,' Douglass instructed. 'Let's have a little talk about what we should do.'

'This is horse crap!' someone yelled.

'Total nonsense!' cried another man.

'Then what can we do?' Douglass interjected patiently.

Nothing, William feared. *They're in charge*.

'Next time the paymaster comes we refuse the money!' someone shouted.

A disapproving rumble went up from the crowd. 'Boo,' said the men, as one.

'Naw, hear me,' the guy said. 'We gotta make sure they know they still owe us. Make sure they know we rejected this half-measure outright.'

Sergeant Major Douglass patted his hands in the air to calm them. 'Indeed, it is wrong what they have done. This man is right. We must stand firm, and demand they pay us what they owe us.' Douglass paused. 'In fact…' He let the word trail out, like he was thinking about it. 'We have to give *this* money back. We can't have them coming to say we altered our agreement.'

The booing from the men grew louder, with a low hiss underneath.

'Think about it,' Douglass said. 'We accept *half* of what they owe us this time, they're gonna come back with *half* again next time.'

'You think they're paying white soldiers half?' someone called out. 'Heck no! They'd walk, and so should we.'

'We are not quitting,' Douglass said. 'We can protest, but the cause at hand is worth our fight. We've already served, and they already owe us. Quitting is not the answer.'

'Give it back, then!'

'Yeah, give it back!'

The murmurs of distress slowly gave way to passionate shouts of protest.

The sergeant major paced before the men. 'White soldiers get thirteen dollars *plus* a clothing allowance, not minus. Did you know that?'

The men booed.

'This is all kinds of unfair.' Douglass raised his fist. 'I say, we boycott.'

'We should take no pay?' someone shouted. 'No way! We fighting to *not* be slaves no more.'

'Exactly,' answered Douglass. 'We are not enslaved. We don't have to take this pittance. We deserve to be paid.'

'That's just perfect for them,' another man piped up. 'They got us *volunteering* to not get paid now? Shoot.'

Douglass shook his head. 'Refusing the pay doesn't mean never getting paid. It means holding out for what they promised. It means not compromising, not accepting their lies.'

William crouched among the others, his heart beating hard. The cash in his hand was a lot of money. Money to care for his father. Money to help free his mother. Giving it back was unthinkable. And yet...

The army had broken their word. The government had either lied outright about their plans to pay equally, or they had decided to renege. Either option was bad.

Ultimately William stood back in line with the others. Freedom meant equality, for Americans. If soldiers couldn't have it, how could anyone? He plunked his money down before the paymaster.

'William Carney,' he said. 'I will wait until the army can pay me what I'm owed in full.'

It felt good to take a stand. It felt good to have a choice. The soldier making so much noise earlier had been wrong. This wasn't a return to enslavement. This was their fight to be free.

A FATE WORSE THAN DEATH

The 54th infantry stood at attention as Colonel Shaw climbed on a stack of crates to address them. Everything fell absolutely still. The colonel hovered silently above them for a long moment before speaking. 'It has come to my attention that you men have not been properly paid.'

William held his breath. Was this going to be the moment when they learned it was a mistake to return their pay?

'Your protest has been noted,' the colonel continued. 'I would like you to know I have written to my superiors seeking remedy for the situation. This is wrong.' Shaw stood tall, flicking his moustache with his thumb. 'What the army just tried to do to you is *wrong*.'

The men stood silent, as their training demanded. William glanced around out of the corners of his eyes. Were they all bursting with sudden pride, with recognition, as he was?

'You have chosen to stay and fight, despite this underhandedness, and for that you have shown great honour.' Shaw cleared his throat.

William strained to catch a glance at the officers clustered around him.

'Now, there is a bit of additional news that bears on your service,' the colonel said. 'We have received a report from the Confederates. They have learned of the existence of this regiment, and they, like I, can see your potential to advance the Union cause.' Shaw clasped his hands behind his back, in that regal and commanding way the officers all seemed to mimic but could not match. 'Naturally they do not agree with our choice to have coloureds among our ranks, and they have declared that if coloured soldiers are captured in uniform they will be subject to an immediate return to slavery.'

William gasped softly. He quickly bit back the sound.

'Also, they will not take any prisoners from this unit. If I or my officers are taken, we will be executed simply for standing in command of coloured troops.' Shaw paused for a long moment, tapping his moustache. 'This new information poses a great dilemma for us all.'

William's mind raced. Death was always a possibility for a soldier, he knew that. But a return to enslavement? To be back in bondage, subject to another man's whims? *You're walking straight back into their hands*, his father had said. Perhaps he was right. The risk was even greater than William had initially realized. After having known freedom, after standing in the sun and the rain on his own terms, to have it ripped away? Some men might say that fate was worse than dying free.

A short while later, William was moving supply crates from a wagon to the cooking area, thinking about the colonel's announcement. He'd offered the men and the officers alike the chance to resign from service, if they felt this new risk was too great.

But none had left. The threat of re-enslavement hadn't seemed to matter to most of the men. They had already chosen to put their lives on the line. However, William couldn't help wondering what could happen. It's not like he'd be returned to Norfolk, to someplace familiar. He'd be sold, no doubt, perhaps sent to pick cotton or tobacco, far from the sight of the sea.

He thought about what his father might say, and how to write to him about it. Whether to speak about this at all. He probably wouldn't. It was easier to talk to his father about the ways he was serving, not the things he feared. Those things would only prove his father was right. Maybe he didn't have what it took to succeed in the Union Army.

William hefted another crate from the wagon and lugged it through the shadows at the edge of the cooking area. Footsteps and voices approached.

'Shaw really turned that around,' one officer was saying.

'Does he believe what comes out of his mouth?' The second officer chuckled.

'He might just,' the first officer confirmed. 'You know he went above Montgomery's head, telling the army to actually use them? If Shaw and Lincoln have their way, these coloureds might see the front lines someday after all.'

'Best send them to the front,' the second officer said. 'First *on* the ground means first *in* the ground, eh?'

'We'll see how many of them even stick around to fight now.' There was a pause.

William held still in the shadows. Had they seen him? The officers might not particularly like to know they were being overheard, even though he was just doing his duty.

'I don't know,' said the first officer. 'If they were going to pay them less they should have said so up front. They would've taken it. No harm, no foul. That was the army's real mistake.'

After the voices faded, William continued moving the crates. He shook his head. He had known men who spoke out of both sides of their mouths before, but this fight was about their lives. Their freedom. They had no choice but to trust these leaders, who clearly did not see them as men.

Chester came charging up. 'There you are. Haven't you heard? We're packing up! They're sending us to join an assault on a Confederate fort.'

'We'll be in position to actually join the battle,' Ephraim added. 'Finally!'

The officers' words floated back to William. *First on the ground means first in the ground.*

'That's great,' he said, but suddenly the fear was winning. He tried to shake it off. He wanted the chance to fight, to prove himself. He still wanted to make a difference in this war, to stomp on the Confederacy with one big Union boot. So why was his stomach roiling and his skin pricking with something sharper than sweat? Why was his mind plagued by thoughts of re-enslavement and the fear of men falling, struck by a bullet he had fired?

They packed up their bedrolls and stocked their food pouches with hardtack and salt pork. They marched. The regiment boarded a pair of steamers, much to Ephraim's dismay, and rode out to the islands off the coast.

The 54th regiment landed on James Island and set up camp. From here, the officers told them, they would be positioned to defend against further Confederate approaches to Morris Island, where the Confederate stronghold of Fort Wagner stood.

One day soon they would storm the ramparts and try to take the fort.

11

IN THE THICK OF IT

16th July 1863

The officers spoke of Fort Wagner with reverence. It was a beast of a place, built into the hillside at the ocean edge of Morris Island. From its forward position, it defended Charleston Harbour. On one side, Wagner was rimmed by a narrow strip of beach. On the other, thick marshland, impossible to traverse. Union forces had tried to take the fort several weeks before and failed. Formidable, to say the least. Impenetrable, according to some rumours.

The assault plan seemed immense, with multiple regiments playing a role. The plan, as William understood it, was to attack simultaneously from land and sea, to send infantry up the beaches and onto the hillside to climb the parapet, while booming cannons off ships and attacking from multiple sides.

They were in the thick of it now. Their new camp on James Island was no kind of refuge from the impending sense of the battle. The companies sent out to picket reported small skirmishes nightly. The sound of cannons and gunfire permeated the air. Regularly, if not constantly. An ever-present reminder that danger lurked just beyond view.

The promise of battle seemed exciting to many, now inevitable to all. It became hard to imagine that they had ever feared not seeing action, for now it was all around them. It was everything.

When it was William's turn to patrol on the picket line, it no longer felt like an exercise. Training was over. At any time, the enemy could advance. If they did, he would be on the front lines. William stood guard with his rifle for hours at the outskirts of camp. Watching. Waiting. Ready to warn the others of an impending threat. It was exhausting, but there was no rest. He tried to barely blink for fear of missing something.

He leaned against a tree and thought back to the tale he'd spun for Alex on their first night in training camp. Now, as he hovered in the shadows keeping watch, he knew he had gotten it wrong. His body vibrated with tension, not from what he could see, but from what he couldn't. Not from what was approaching, but from what he feared might be out there. Here and now, imagining the whites of the enemy's eyes was irrelevant. His fear of taking aim with such certainty seemed small in comparison to all there was to fear of the unknown.

He came off duty in the late afternoon, gradually lowering his guard and relaxing back into the relative safety of numbers within the camp. As the sun went down, rifle shots echoed off the surrounding trees, closer than he had ever heard. William and the others around him ran for their rifles. The gunfire was close, possibly even approaching. It continued for quite a while.

This was more than a skirmish. They were under attack.

Even as the sounds of battle continued, soldiers began trickling back from the front. In camp now there was a hospital tent, set up to care for the wounded. Survivors of the few brief skirmishes bore bandages stained with blood and told stories of the heat and smoke of constant rifle fire. They had lost several dozen of their number in battle to boot, but Company C had yet to see any action. Chester constantly lamented this, and William nodded along, ashamed of the relief he felt over not being tested.

His father's warning about his softness returned to haunt him.

The main assault was but a few days away, William guessed. He wasn't sure. No one told them exactly how long, perhaps to keep it a surprise as long as possible, in case anyone from the regiment was captured or compromised. Preparations had increased tenfold. Officers scurried about looking busy and thoughtful, while the men lugged crates, cleared land and drilled and drilled to near exhaustion.

William's cartridge pouch was now fully stocked with the little paper envelopes of powder and Minié balls he'd need when the time came to fire. The unit drilled and practised as they had for these last months.

When it was time to move out, the weather turned damp and chilly. They left camp in the dusk and marched, not the way they had come, just one short mile from the coast, but towards the far side of James Island. A long, four-mile hike, in the rain, in the dark.

On a good day, in training, covering four miles on foot was but a blink. They had trained so hard they could walk for ever, on a good day. This was night, and a bad one.

William slipped and slid through mud, barely able to keep his footing. The uneven terrain and narrow paths threatened to get the best of them, over and over. He wiped water from his face with an equally damp wrist. His uniform jacket clung soggily to him, weighing him down even more, as did his dripping pack and the rapidly disintegrating hardtack in his food pouch.

They climbed through murky swamps, over slick bridges, balancing along logs, often walking single file. Two by two, at most. William was forced to put aside all thought of the impending battle. It required all his concentration to keep his focus on placing one foot in front of the other.

He struggled to stay upright. The march was awful. Miserable. The muck and the rain and the rotting stench of swamp grass pushed all the worst thoughts to the front of his mind.

Too soft. Too soft. Too soft…

You don't have what it takes to be a soldier.

Too soft. Too soft. Too soft…

You're still a Black man. They won't forget it.

Did these officers even know where they were leading the men? Would they be lost for ever in this dark wilderness? Even if they emerged from this place, scratched and bitten and filthy, what was to become of them? *The first on the ground means the first in the ground.* The words echoed, and the men's casual laughter.

These officers did not care about them. Coloured soldiers were either useless or expendable. *Why are we following them? We are better than this. We are more than what they can see in us.*

Mosquitoes, splashing mud, aching feet, straining eyes to keep view of the back of the man in front of him… William felt mired in horror throughout the trek.

They're going to kill us, his mind whispered. *They are leading us to our death.*

It took all night to cross the island. The light had begun to pink the horizon by the time they reached the shore. Waiting for them, a pair of steamer ships, painted with *Cossack* and *Chasseur*.

'All aboard,' urged the captain. 'Let's go, let's go.'

'Boats, again,' Ephraim groaned, wringing water out of his sleeves as they waited their turn to mount the boarding plank.

A soldier standing near them pointed at the dark blur of land across the inlet. 'One last boat ride,' he said. 'That's Morris Island. That's where we'll make history.'

The men craned their necks. The legend of Fort Wagner loomed large. Maybe to see it would render it real, not so much larger than life. They could see the island, but not the fort itself. There was more trekking ahead.

History, William thought. He glanced up at the white faces of the officers striding around looking bossy and important. Shivers of fear and mistrust rattled through him. *Will we* make *history, or* be *history?*

A RESTLESS NIGHT

William huddled around the smallest of fires with Ephraim and Chester. They were taking advantage of a break in the rain to try to get warm, or at least somewhat drier. Across the circle, a group of other soldiers were arguing.

'Ain't you heard them officers?' one man was saying. He had his knees pulled up to his chest, rocking slightly. 'They think we're good for nothing.'

'They ain't tryin' to hide it,' answered a man gnawing on a small stick.

'Yeah, they call themselves the coloured keepers.' The third man chuckled, firelight illuminating the gap between his front teeth.

'They love to talk about how they volunteered to be our officers. Like they the greatest freedom-loving

89

people you ever met. Shoot.' The rocking man rocked harder.

They kept their voices to a loud whisper so as not to be overheard. William was at once relieved to know he was not alone in his thoughts and fears, and suddenly more deeply worried about their situation.

'But they know we never gonna see serious action,' said the man with the stick. 'I think they volunteered to protect their own behinds from the line of fire.'

'Next thing you know they'll have us cooking and cleaning for some white soldiers somewhere,' said rocking man. 'We about to be some house soldiers.' They laughed.

Suddenly there was a commotion at the edge of the circle. 'It's the colonel,' someone whispered. Men started scrambling to their feet.

'At ease,' Colonel Shaw said. 'Keep your seats.'

The soldiers nearest him scooted out of the way just the same. Shaw crouched in the mud amid their circle.

'How are you doing, men?' he asked.

An awkward chorus of 'oh, fine', 'yes, sir', 'we good' sorts of rumbles came up.

'Tomorrow is a big day for all of us,' Shaw said quietly. 'Can you feel that?'

Similar rumbles rolled across the circle again.

'I know that all of this feels like an uphill battle,' the colonel said. 'Tomorrow it will be that indeed.

We will lead the charge. I want you to know that whatever you have heard, whatever has been said, whatever the rest of the army or the country might think of you. Of *us*' – he paused, emphasizing again – 'of *us*… Whatever people might think of us, I believe in you. I believe in my bones that tomorrow we will take the field and walk away with nothing less than full glory. You are the strongest, bravest regiment I have been a privilege to be a part of.'

'Why'd you volunteer to lead a coloured unit?' the man with the stick called out.

'I was asked,' Shaw said. 'And it seemed rightly time for such a thing.'

'How come?'

Shaw turned up his hands. 'My family are abolitionists,' he said. 'We believe no man should be subject to another man. Not if this country prides itself on freedom.'

'We heard you had to demand our chance to fight.' The men seemed to be growing more comfortable with the idea of talking again. William watched the firelight flicker shadows over Colonel Shaw's face. The army had reneged on their pay, long held them back from fighting, and would now send them in as the first against a fortress some said was impenetrable.

William studied Shaw closely. Black men rising up with guns to fight for freedom is what white men had always feared. Was this man, this officer, truly any different from the others? When push came to shove, would Shaw sacrifice honour for power like so many of his brothers?

Shaw lowered his head and stroked his moustache. 'It is my belief that you are as well-trained and competent as any army unit I've ever witnessed. As such, you deserve the chance to do what they sent you here to do.'

'So now you're sending us to the front?'

'Our assignment is to lead the charge into battle,' Shaw said. 'We are going to take this fort.'

As a group, the men around the fire sat up a little taller. *Lead the charge?* William thought. In the light glow of the flames, the faces around him exchanged glances full of similar surprise.

Shaw got to his feet. 'Make me proud, men. As you were.' He strode off into the darkness, seemingly headed to join another group of soldiers. Perhaps he planned to speak to every man in the regiment. If so, William thought, that was something.

He sighed, leaning his back against Chester's again. Colonel Shaw seemed like a good person, perhaps more calm and steady than the other officers. Perhaps that's why he was in charge. William wanted to believe him when he said he had faith in their regiment, but he knew all too well the kinds of things officers said behind the soldiers' backs. And sometimes to their faces.

None of these officers, perhaps even Shaw, saw the coloured men as equals. They were all but pawns in a very large and deadly game of chess between two great powers who, by rights, should have been one. This war that pitted brother against brother also pitted the nation against itself. It pitted the idea of freedom for people like him against the idea that white men making money and having power was all that mattered in the world.

William clasped his hands, offering up a small prayer for the strength of their regiment. Tomorrow, they would fight. Tomorrow they would stand proud under the Stars and Stripes. He offered a prayer for his friends by name, for Colonel Shaw and the officers to show smart leadership, for all the regiments they would meet, for the Confederates they would strive to defeat – for his father, to soothe his worries.

He offered a final prayer for himself, for strength and courage to override this fear knocking at the base of his heart. He would not, could not, be too soft for this war. Not when it mattered most.

'MAKE ME PROUD, MEN!'

18th July 1863

Williams's stomach rumbled. There had been no food and little rest during the recent journey. He marched in formation, across the sand in the centre of a row of men. The assault on Fort Wagner from Union artillery, both land and sea, was already underway. The boom of cannons, the snap of rifle shot from skirmish fire came at regular intervals.

The 54th would be the first wave of the ground assault from the beach side of the fort. As they prepared to emerge from behind the cover of trees and march onto the narrow stretch of sand between the ocean and the fort, William's gut tightened. His first real glimpse of battle would come at any moment.

Sergeant Major Douglass paced in front of

William's section. 'We will fight bravely,' he told them. 'Today we will show what a unit of Black men can be.' He looked at the sky, then back at his company. 'I believe this moment is ordained,' he told them. 'God be with each of you.'

William clutched his rifle tighter. His hands had become sweat-slicked already in the warm July air. He flared his nostrils wide, smelling the salt from the sea. He thought of himself months ago, back home in New Bedford, up on the mast of the whaling ship, breathing freedom. The blue-grey ocean America he imagined was a sight for sore eyes.

William pressed his shoulder against Chester's, briefly. Just a nudge of encouragement. Chester's wide, eager face glanced back at him.

'Here we go,' his friend whispered. 'See you on the other side.'

William swallowed hard. He was sure Chester meant the other side of the battle, when all was said and done and the 54th emerged in honoured victory, their colours flying high. But he couldn't help the small stabs of terror that they could meet again on the other side in a different way... in death.

'See you,' he answered.

Chester grinned. 'We're gonna climb that wall and knock their teeth out!'

William couldn't help but smile. Leave it to Chester to put things in colourful terms.

'Men of the 54th!' Colonel Shaw's voice echoed from the front. He stood ahead of the whole regiment, on a slight rise at the spot where the sand began turning to grass. 'I want you to prove yourselves,' the colonel proclaimed. 'The eyes of thousands will look on what you do tonight.'

Then, instead of retreating to the back of the formation, as officers typically did, Shaw took position on the front lines.

'Forward march!'

The officers standing in formation alongside the troops sent a palpable jolt of pride through the unit. This, this is what they were fighting for. The chance to stand on equal ground, with equal footing. To stand up for their nation, for the spirit of freedom together, as men of all races. A man might say and believe all sorts of things, but where he stood when the moment really mattered said something greater than words.

William lifted his knees in time with the other men of the unit. *Hup two three four. Hup two three four.* Moving in unison felt good. They were as ready as they'd ever be. Time to tackle this hill, this fort, this battle for the future of their nation.

Their moment had finally come.

William breathed the sea air. The free air. He prayed that these breaths would not be his last.

Here we go…

14

MARCHING INTO BATTLE

Colonel Shaw led the charge across the beach, the regiment's flags flapping in the breeze alongside him. William could no longer see the colonel past the rows of soldiers ahead of him, but he kept his eye fixed upon the colours. The 54th would do the Union proud, he was certain of it.

They emerged from the cover of trees and marched onto the open beach. Ahead and above them, Fort Wagner loomed from the hillside. The sandy beach gave way to a gently sloping grass-covered rise that formed the fort's ramparts. What he could see looked like more hill than wall, as though the fort was carved right into the side of the island, with just a bit of stone peeking up over the top of the grassy rise.

They had been told that a ten-foot ditch surrounded the fort as well, but from this angle,

William could not see it, only the stone tips jutting up from the grass – the parapet. The Confederate flag flew from the top of the fort. It looked small in the distance, whipping taut for brief moments before falling slack at the whim of the wind.

The men of the 54th regiment strode across the beach, all eyes raised to greet the uphill landscape ahead.

At first, there was quiet. The absence of sound other than William's own heaving breaths and the squawk of spectator gulls soaring over the water. Then the rifle fire rang out, a sound both familiar and entirely new – now that it was so close it could really be coming for him.

The next layer of sound was wholly terrifying. As they drew closer to the fort, cannons boomed from on high.

Cannonballs struck the water, sending up splashing walls of waves.

Cannonballs struck the beach, showering them with grains of sand.

Cannonballs struck the grass, loosening chunks of earth.

Those were the ones that missed. Each cannonball that hit cut a vicious, bullet-like arc through a column of men, knocking them senseless. Their screams added a new layer of sound. William's ears pulsed with it.

'Double time!' shouted the colonel. The soldiers picked up their marching pace. *Hup hup hup hup*.

Suddenly they were marching over fallen men. Many of those on the front lines had been hit. Traversing the uneven sand no longer seemed the challenge it had been a moment ago. The beach became an obstacle course of bodies, some writhing and crying out in pain, some lying all too still and crumpled.

The sight made William want to turn back. He had been at war for a matter of minutes, and already it was too much. Yet he found himself lurching his way across the beach and up the hill towards the fort.

'Charge!' shouted Colonel Shaw.

This was nothing like the skirmish had been. This was not a fair fight on an open field, but a deadly attempt to reach a well-protected enemy. William thought he had known this going in, but living it was different.

The men in the fort were protected by thick stone walls. The men running up the beach were protected only by the bodies of the men in front of them.

Cannonballs and grenades rained down. The company was taking heavy fire.

The goal was simply to run, run. Get up the wall. If they could climb the ramparts and mount the parapet, if *enough* of them could, they could enter the fort. And hopefully fight long enough to claim it.

Run.

Run.

Oof!

William stumbled against the arm of a fallen man. He fell to one knee, the butt of his rifle landing in the dirt beside him. He leaned on it like a crutch, to steady himself.

'William!' Chester appeared at his side, grasping his arm. 'You hit?'

'No, I just tripped,' William answered, lunging back to his feet.

'We have to keep moving,' Chester shouted.

It was hard to hear even the words of someone standing beside him, the force of the battle was so loud.

'Where is Ephraim?' William called. They had planned to run into battle together. They had started together, hadn't they? Plans had begun to give way to chaos.

'I don't know,' Chester answered. 'Maybe he got ahead of us. Come on.'

William raised his rifle, although there was not yet any call to fire. They had to get up, up and over, before they could fight first-hand. The Confederates were behind a wall. His bayonet was fixed. He was ready.

Chester moved ahead, shouting a wordless battle cry. William charged along behind him, scanning the line for the Stars and Stripes. All they had to do was follow the flag.

From somewhere beyond the parapet, a bullet flew towards them. It found a mark.

Chester lurched backward, stung by hot metal.

A FALLEN FRIEND

'Chester!' William shouted as his friend staggered back a few steps, then fell onto the sand. Chester landed awkwardly, half on his side, half on his back, on top of a man already fallen – and dead, for sure. The fallen man's face was pressed all the way into the sand and he was entirely and certainly still.

Blood bloomed from Chester's shoulder. So much blood. Chester threw his arm across his own chest and grasped the place where a bullet was now lodged. Blood leaked between his fingers.

William dropped to his side and pressed his own hand atop Chester's. 'Oh no. Oh God,' he murmured.

'Go,' Chester said, through gritted teeth. 'Fight. I'm OK.'

'But—'

The rest of the 54th was still charging. Around them, over them, through them.

'Just go,' Chester insisted. 'Run!'

'I can't leave you,' William insisted, holding tight to his friend's hand. It was just as noble, wasn't it, to be there for someone in need? Reverend Jackson had tried to convince him of that before he enlisted. Maybe the reverend and his father had been right. Maybe he wasn't meant to be a soldier, but one who stood beside the fallen. One who prayed, one who kept the faith in the midst of the trial. Too soft for war, indeed. 'I won't leave you.'

'You must. Go—' Chester's grip relaxed and his eyes slid shut.

'Chester!' William shouted. More people were falling around them. The fullness of time seemed that it would always be the boom of cannons, the crack of guns. Every sound, loud and scary.

No, no, no. Everything within him was crying, screaming. The unit surged around him, jostling him out of his shock. To stay still was to become an easy target.

Ahead, the Stars and Stripes billowed, calling him back to service. Casting a last glance at Chester, William staggered to his feet and re-joined the charge.

He struggled forward against the uneven slipping of the sand. Nothing but devastation behind him, more destruction ahead. Death lay in the forward charge. It seemed all but certain, judging by the sea of brown skin and blue uniforms laid out before him. But great shame lay in an early retreat – and he had promised his life to the struggle. William gasped for breath, hoping for a hint of the refreshing breeze off the water. Hoping for a hint that the freedom he so longed for – that all his people longed for – was still close at hand.

He licked his sandy lips instinctively, then spit the grossness back out. The air no longer smelled of ocean and salt and freedom. Now it smelled of blood, powder and pain. There was no way out. A kind of trapped he'd never felt before. This fight was the pure opposite of freedom. They were being mown down like so many blades of grass. Soon their bodies would be covered in sand. The winds of time would forget them.

William strode desperately across the sand. In the high distance, the parapet loomed larger than life. What folly, to think that their lines of brown men could ever be a match for such stone. What fools they had all been, throwing their arrogance right in the face of God.

Colonel Shaw's voice rang out from the ramparts. 'Forward, 54th!' he shouted, leading the charge towards the parapet. William fixed his eye on the colonel as he ran. Along the parapet, a row of sparkling flashes of light, like tiny fireworks, burst forth.

Colonel Shaw jolted backward, coming up short as if he had run into a wall. A plume of red mist billowed around his shoulders. William gasped as the colonel stumbled back along the ramparts, before falling limp into the watery ditch below.

'Colonel Shaw!' someone screamed. Many someones, perhaps.

William's stomach roiled, but he choked back his horror and tried to move forward. With their leader fallen, who could they look to now? He scanned the front lines for the bold Union colours. There. There was the flag. The sight had drawn him up from Chester's side, and it would keep him going.

Keep courage, he reminded himself.

He ran.

There was young John Wall, bearing the flag, directly ahead of William, closer than he could have imagined. Keep courage, indeed.

William had made such good progress that he was nearing the front lines. He kept his eye on the flapping standard. If he kept focus on only that, he could do this. Never mind the terror. Never mind the fallen. He could be the soldier he was supposed to be, the one charged by the Governor of Massachusetts, by the President of the United States, to do his duty in service of freedom for all.

Suddenly the flag dipped and swerved. A few yards ahead of William, John stumbled. William could see he had been hit. Bleeding. He was going to fall!

John's arms dropped slack to his sides, releasing the flagpole.

The flag, the precious Union colours…

William dropped his rifle. He leaped forward and caught John with one arm. He grabbed the flagpole with the other.

'John!' William cried.

But there was no hope. John slipped out of his arms, shot through the heart and already motionless. William watched in horror as the flag bearer hit the ground.

No! The colours – who would carry the colours?

William spun round, as if to search for the rest of the colour guard, someone to take up the colours. And then he realized. Already in his own hands, the flag remained aloft.

KEEPING THE COLOURS ALOFT

The air closed tight around William. The thought that he could flee, or hide, or flop to the earth in surrender suddenly evaporated. He stood at the centre of things, in a way he hadn't been just moments ago.

His sweat-slicked, sand-caked fingers locked around the flagpole in his hands. The precious Union colours. Holding the flag was an honour, a privilege of which he was not worthy. He glanced around. Who was supposed to take up the flag?

But there was no one. The men nearest him struggled forth. Few, it seemed, kept their feet for long. They sprawled, adding to the bloody piles. Shouts of warning, screams of agony rent the air.

William stood fast.

'*Before it shall ever be surrendered to the foes may its*

white stripes be spattered with the red blood of those who bear it in the field.' William was struck by the memory of Governor Andrew's words, when he had handed over the flag to Colonel Shaw.

Colonel Shaw, now fallen on this very field.

'*This banner has never been surrendered to the foe. Hold onto the staff, if every thread is blown away, your glory will be the same.*'

The words had meant so much that day in Boston, but they meant even more here and now. Here, among the fallen, their red blood spattered. Now, with the flag itself tattered and shredded by the teeth of this battle.

But it was still their flag.

William stood frozen beneath the Stars and Stripes. Amid the swirling chaos, this one thing absorbed him – holding fast, keeping the colours aloft.

Around him, the 54th regiment's charge seemed to be faltering, but it couldn't stop. It couldn't.

The task to take the fort had been given to them. They could not fail.

He had no rifle any more. He must have cast it aside instinctively when he took up the flagpole. He was no longer in a position to fight, but the battle must continue.

Holding the flag, William suddenly realized he had been charged with something. *As goes the flag, so go the soldiers.*

The faltering advance rested on his own shoulders. The tide of this battle was his to turn around.

Gripping the pole with renewed energy, William strode forward, through the fog of musket smoke. With his hands occupied by the flag, it was harder than ever to keep his balance along the uneven sand. It should have been similar to carrying the rifle, but somehow it wasn't. His task was suddenly so much bigger. He struggled through the now-familiar obstacle course of fallen men.

'Hold the line,' he shouted. 'To the parapet!'

He did not know if the men around him could hear his cry, but by God, they could see the colours. His climb was slow but fierce. All context fell away, save the struggle forward, upward.

As he ascended, his fear, too, slipped away. Everything was different now. That which he had been preparing for and dreading all these months was no longer his test. Did he have the courage of conviction to fire his rifle in battle? Could he muster the ruthlessness to stab a man in the heart? It no longer mattered.

For the test he now faced, William knew full well he had all the strength he needed. Courage, faith, hope, a vision of freedom that transcended the ways of this land as he knew it. This, he had in spades.

And the flag represented it all.

'Forward!' he shouted. The 54th could not back down and still do honour to the colours that he carried. William gripped the pole with renewed energy and ran forward, even as he felt his skin catch fire, bullets tearing through him.

17

HUZZAH! HUZZAH!

He was alone. The haze of battle faded to a dull grey roar around him.

He was alone, save for the flag.

His body felt afire. His arm stung, blood running down his bicep, dripping from his elbow. He had been shot.

Still he climbed. He could see the surface now, the crest of the parapet. He could get there. He would stand atop the fort and wave the Stars and Stripes, urging the men forward.

The burning pain had spread to his leg now. William tried to ignore the gash in his thigh, from a second bullet. *Forget the pain*, he told himself. As long as he *could* still walk, he had to.

He found himself boldly leading the advance. It wasn't really up to him, he began to feel – the flag was driving itself. The flag wanted to fly as high as it could.

Finally, William climbed over the top of the ramparts, placing the flagpole firmly atop the parapet of the enemy fort. He had done it!

Gritting his teeth against the pain in his limbs, he hoisted the flag even higher, waving it like a beacon. The men would follow.

For a brief, shining moment, it appeared the 54th had gained the upper hand. His fellow soldiers poured over the ramparts, bayonets affixed. For that brief moment, it seemed they were taking the fort!

A column of men rushed towards him, and William waved the flag harder, drawing them to his defence. *Huzzah! Huzzah!*

The victorious feeling was, however, fleeting.

The wall of soldiers surging towards him were clad in grey, not blue.

He was about to be surrounded.

He was alone, save for the flag. And the flag was a prime target. Rifle fire exploded toward him. He could not let the colours fall into enemy hands!

William leaped away from the parapet, racing down the embankment.

He landed in the water-filled ditch. The water rose to his chest, sucking him down!

William grabbed the tip of the flag and wrapped it tightly around the pole, keeping it above water.

He splashed free of the ditch and crouched against the base of the hill that formed the fort wall. He hunkered down, making himself small, keeping the flag aloft. The flag could not fall. It would not fall.

The battle raged around him. His chest burned too, now. How much longer could he last in this onslaught? His wounds bled fiercely and his core and limbs alike screamed in agony.

William sank down and curled himself around the flagpole, bracing it tightly with his body. He would become a hill of his own, if that was what it took to do his duty.

A fresh, intense conviction shone through the pain, buoying him beneath the darkening sky. *Too soft for war?* No longer. He would hold fast. Firm as the wall itself. Hard as a stone. Impenetrable.

He vowed that even if *he* fell, the flag would not fall.

VICTORIOUS RETREAT

Williiam felt hands grasping his shoulders. He raised his head. Two white faces gazed down at him with concern.

'I will never surrender!' William shouted at them. There was no bayonet within reach. His world was the flagpole. If he died on this hill it would be in service of the Union. *Let there be blood on the flag before it falls to the enemy...*

'Sure, buddy,' said one of them, 'But we've been ordered to retreat. Quickly, now.'

That's when William realized – they were Union soldiers too. The back-up regiments must have arrived to continue the fight! There was still hope...

'Are we winning?' he asked.

'We're retreating,' answered one of the men, louder this time. The pair was still working to drag the flag-bearer-turned-cornerstone to his feet. 'They had more reinforcements than we expected.'

'Come on,' urged the other. He took hold of William's left elbow. 'We have to get out of here. Now!'

William unfolded himself. Standing was hard. His shot leg burned as if someone was holding a flame to it. The white soldiers hoisted and supported him. *Strange*, thought William, as he limped away from the ramparts. *I am alive.*

'Let me carry the flag for you,' said the man on his right.

William clung to the flagpole. He tried to shake his head, but the motion sent searing pain through his neck. He fought to speak through the pain, over the deafening, never-ending boom of rifle and cannon fire. 'No one but a member of the 54th should carry the colours,' he finally whispered.

The white soldier's eyes widened in surprise, but he stopped trying to wrest the flagpole from William. Instead, the soldier gripped the young flag bearer with both hands and tried to ease the weight on his injured leg.

Boom. Boom.

Through squinted eyes, William caught slices of the battle. Or, it seemed, the retreat. The soldiers still up and moving seemed mostly white. The second wave of the advance had clearly begun.

As they picked their way down the hill, they stepped over and around dozens of fallen men. Brown faces with eyes staring unseeingly upward. Brown hands resting still against rifle wood. Brown cheeks pressed into the sand.

William was struck with a terrible thought: was he all that was left of his 54th regiment?

'Who are you with?' William asked the white soldiers.

'The 100th New York,' said the guy on his right, panting with exertion.

Boom.

The soldier at his left yelped a curse. The trio stumbled but kept their footing.

William could taste blood all of a sudden. It was streaming down the side of his face. His head throbbed and his temple stung.

'God,' said the white soldier. 'You're hit in the head, and you're still upright.'

'The colours,' William murmured, as the edges of his vision grew dark. He focused on his fingers, slick with sweat and blood and mud and peppered with sand, still gripping the flagpole. The flag itself was out of his sight now, but he imagined it streaming high. *Carry the pole…*

Somehow, he kept walking. This time, he would not be the small one in the back of the crowd. This time, he would not give up too soon. This time, he would not doubt himself. This time, he was unafraid.

A crowd of brown faces greeted him. The 54th! The men jumped and cheered, waving him on to safety, but William's ears were only ringing with the sounds of the battle.

'You can let go now,' said one of the white soldiers. 'This is your regiment.'

'Get this man to the hospital tent,' said the other. 'He's got wounds in his head, chest, arms and leg.'

A Black soldier William didn't recognize lifted the pole from his hands. 'We have it now,' he said. 'You brought it back to us. Amazing.'

William allowed his fingers to relax. Letting go felt right now, and good. His body gave way and he began to collapse. Many hands buoyed William as his eyes slipped shut. He fought for a moment to open them, gazing up at his regiment mates.

'Boys, I only did my duty,' he said. 'The old flag never touched the ground.'

THE COST OF FREEDOM

William woke up some time later, immediately warm in the stifling afternoon heat. He blinked up at the white ceiling of the hospital tent, trying to place his surroundings. His body ached. His face and arm were bandaged. To move at all made his chest ache like it was being hammered.

'This one's coming round,' said a voice somewhere nearby.

'So he is.' Hands touched his arm. 'I'm right here, son,' said a gentle voice.

'Dad?' William whispered. His throat was parched. It was hard to speak.

The voice laughed lightly. A voice, William suddenly realized, that was decidedly female.

'We're gonna do what we can to make sure you

make it home to him,' the woman said. Her hands moved over him, checking his wounds. 'My name is Martha. What's yours?'

'Carney,' he answered. 'William Carney.'

'Glad you're still with us, Sergeant Carney,' Martha said. 'Now, take a sip.' She placed her hand under his neck, gently lifting his head. The rim of a tin cup tapped his lips, sloshing cool water into his mouth. William drank gratefully.

'Are we still at war?' he asked.

Martha smiled. 'Certainly so.'

William flushed, embarrassed. 'Yes. No, I mean, is the battle over? Do I need to go back to the field?' He tried to sit up.

Martha patted his hand gently, while holding his shoulder down against the table, not so gently. 'You need to rest. The battle has been over for a day already. Don't you worry. There'll be others.' Her tone was at once long-suffering and matter-of-fact.

'Do you want to write to your father?' Martha asked. 'We can get you paper, and someone to write it.'

'I can write it,' William said. 'I should write it.' He thought about the letters he had already sent, so full of hope and determination. So insistent that the fight was right. Now, he felt a weight on him. The weight of all he had seen, and what he had done.

Exhaustion overtook him. Later. He could write to his father later.

But when he closed his eyes, he saw flashes along the parapet. When he breathed, he feared the sting of the bullets would never go away. The subdued chatter of the other men in the hospital tent echoed their battle screams.

He spied Sergeant Major Douglass across the hospital tent, nursing some sort of injury. Where were Ephraim and Alex? William wondered. Chester... William closed his eyes against the pain of losing his best friend. Chester, most likely, had not survived his wound. There had been so much blood. The flag bearer, John Wall, was dead. Colonel Shaw was surely, too. And many others. Nearly three hundred others dead or missing, according to the whispers. That was nearly half their number. Was this truly the cost of freedom? Today, the price seemed exceptionally steep.

'There you are, old chap,' said a voice, when William next awoke. He opened his eyes and found Chester sitting on the end of his cot. He had a pocketknife in one hand, awkwardly whittling at a stick held fast between his knees. His other arm was bound to his chest in a sling.

'Chester! You're alive?' William gently embraced his friend. They jokingly compared wounds – Chester's single shot was more severe, but William had five! It didn't really matter. They had fought together, and now were scarred together. They had survived.

'Have you seen Ephraim?' William asked.

Chester's eyes clouded. 'He's on the list.'

The list of fallen? *No. Ephraim.* William closed his eyes, feeling a new kind of ache in his chest.

'And Alex?' William was afraid to know, but he had to ask.

'He's all right, somehow. Have you heard them talking about us?' Chester asked. 'They say we done ourselves proud.'

'We did,' William said. 'We made a stand.'

He felt a surge of energy. The moment had come, and they had proved themselves worthy. He had stepped up in the face of war, at once fearless and terrified. He had done it.

'Didn't take the fort, though.'

William gazed into the afternoon light. 'Some of them weren't sure we even could fight. Now they've seen we'll go all the way. Full devotion.'

You were wrong, Dad. We are none of us soft.

Chester nodded. 'You can see it in their eyes. Everything is different now.'

That evening, William and Chester stood outside the hospital tent with the others who were mobile enough. Their new commanding officer, Colonel Hallowell, addressed the troops.

He said, 'The officers and I have written to the army command, as well as to Governor Andrew, and to President Lincoln, to report on the bravery shown these last days by the soldiers of the 54th Massachusetts Regiment. Many of our number have fallen, Colonel Shaw included. May they rest in peace.'

Colonel Hallowell clasped his hands behind his back, as if in homage to Colonel Shaw. William wondered whether it was intentional.

'Also, I've just seen a newspaper article that will be published in the coming days, proclaiming this regiment as heroes of the war. The entire nation will soon know what this coloured regiment did here. Never forget – this battle may go down in history as a defeat, but for one proud moment, our flag flew above that parapet.'

William pulled back his shoulders – *ow* – and tried to stand tall. The commander was speaking of him. At the time, though, it had not felt like an act of pride or power. He had felt desperate, he had clung to the only symbol that seemed to mean anything in the face of all the chaos. At the time, he had still feared he was softer than the others, and helpless.

Except… now he saw it differently. He was not a hero. He hadn't leaped over the wall and confronted a dozen enemies like some of the men. But perhaps it was not always about being big or heroic, but doing his small part, whatever it was, over and over. Perhaps even a soft-hearted man could make the hard choice to stand firm in the face of tyranny.

This time, he had found a way to fight that didn't cause him to enact cruelty. The next time, he might well have to pull a trigger or wield a bayonet, like so many others had done on the hillside at Wagner. He understood that, but all the same the sense of calling that he had felt to be here, to fight, made more sense now. They were changing the country. They were changing what it meant to stand up and fight. The powers that be might say they lost this battle, but in a different way, they had actually won.

'Never forget what you have done here, and the country will never forget what they have seen here,' Hallowell concluded.

Afterwards, William and Chester returned to their cots in silence. William thought about the letter he'd write to his father, that he now could truly say he had made a difference. This one battle was already changing the way the country viewed coloured soldiers. They had proven themselves. They had made a stand. Finally the chance had come, and they had not squandered it. *Huzzah*.

'I saw that flag, you know,' Chester said quietly. 'When I was wounded, at the moment when

I thought I would have to lie in the mud for ever, I saw that flag, and I pulled myself up.'

'Yeah,' said William. 'I saw it too.'

Chester guffawed. 'You lie! The story is making its way around camp, you know.'

'The story?'

'You didn't see the flag,' Chester said. 'You carried it.'

William looked away from the rows of cots full of wounded men. He gazed beyond the tent, through the trees, across the water, into the setting sun. The war was nowhere near over. The colours would fly again and again, no doubt carried by many hands.

'Admit it,' Chester nudged. 'That was you.'

'It was me,' William answered. 'I carried it.'

WHAT HAPPENED NEXT...

TURNING THE TIDE OF THE WAR

The 54th Massachusetts regiment lost many men in their attempt to capture Fort Wagner. Nearly half of the six hundred soldiers who took the field were killed, injured or missing when the battle was done. Confederate soldiers gathered the fallen and buried them in a mass grave, placing the white officers alongside their Black enlisted men. They believed this action represented the highest insult, but even Colonel Shaw's own father acknowledged that it was right for his son to be buried alongside the men he had championed.

In the weeks and months after the battle, newspaper accounts regaled Americans with the story of the 54th Massachusetts regiment's strength and conviction on the battlefield. Their courageous actions at Fort Wagner helped convince the Union Army that Black soldiers could be good for the war effort. Over the final two years of the Civil War, nearly 180,000 Black men enlisted, forming ten per cent of the Union's fighting force. Their participation turned the tide of the war and helped the North secure victory.

It took another full year after Wagner, however, before Congress authorized Black soldiers to be paid on an equal basis with white soldiers. Fortunately, when the order was finally issued, it was deemed retroactive, such that Black soldiers could receive the back pay they were owed.

The American Civil War is generally considered to have ended on 9th April 1865, when Confederate General Robert E. Lee surrendered at the Battle of Appomattox Court House. However, this pivotal moment was followed by several months of de-escalation and continued skirmishing as word of the Union victory slowly spread through the South.

Black soldiers continued to serve in the U.S. Army after the end of the Civil War; however, white and Black soldiers remained in separate units through World War Two. Through the mid-twentieth century, most Black enlisted units were relegated to service assignments, such as ferrying supplies, digging ditches, or working as cleaners and cooks, rather than being allowed to fight. The few Black units who did see action were frequently sent to the front lines, assigned particularly dangerous missions, and otherwise placed in harm's way ahead of white soldiers.

The second-class treatment of Black soldiers, coupled with the second-class treatment of Black Americans back home, highlighted the paradox of the United States as a noble defender of freedom for all around the globe while oppressing a huge swathe of its own citizens. Post-war, these racial frustrations boiled over, helping to fuel the civil rights movement of the 1950s and 1960s, in which Black Americans fought for full integration in all aspects of life and society.

William Carney received an honourable discharge in 1864 due to the leg wound he received in the assault on Fort Wagner. He returned to New Bedford, where he worked various jobs, primarily serving as a mail carrier for many years.

On 23rd May 1900, he received the Medal of Honor for his actions that fateful day on Morris Island. He is often referred to as the first Black recipient of the Medal of Honor, though this is a slightly confusing distinction. Fifteen other Black Civil War soldiers also received the Medal of Honor, and a few received their physical medals earlier than William did. However, the actions that earned Sergeant Carney the honour occurred first in history.

TIMELINE

29th February 1840	William Harvey Carney born in Norfolk, Virginia.
November 1860	Abolitionist Abraham Lincoln elected president of the United States.
20th December 1860	South Carolina secedes from the Union, soon joined by six other states.
4th February 1861	The seven secessionist states meet to form the Confederate States of America. (Ultimately, eleven states would join the Confederacy.)
12th April 1961	Confederate forces fire on Fort Sumter, marking the start of the Civil War.
1st January 1863	President Lincoln issues the Emancipation Proclamation, freeing enslaved people and making it legal for Black men to serve in the armed forces.
January 1863	Massachusetts Governor John Andrew begins recruiting for a Black regiment.
4th March 1863	Carney enlists in the Morgan Guards, Company C of the 54th Massachusetts Regiment Volunteers.
March-May 1863	The 54th regiment trains at Camp Meigs in Readville, Massachusetts.

13th May 1863	The 54th regiment is mustered into federal service.
18th May 1863	Governor Andrew presents the 54th regiment with their unit flags in a public ceremony in Boston. In fact, Governor Andrew and Colonel Shaw's speeches on p.59 are taken from the historical transcript of this occasion.
28th May 1863	The 54th regiment departs on the *DeMolay* steamer out of Boston Harbour.
3rd June 1863	The 54th regiment arrives in Hilton Head, South Carolina.
11th June 1863	The 54th regiment participates minimally in a raid on Darien, Georgia, after which Col. James Montgomery ordered the town burned.
16th June 1863	The Union Army attempts to capture Charleston; members of the 54th regiment fight in supportive skirmishes.
8th July 1863	The 54th regiment are posted on James Island in preparation for the assault on Fort Wagner.
16th July 1863	Members of the 54th fight at Grimball's Landing on James Island.
18th July 1863	The 54th Massachusetts regiment leads the assault on Fort Wagner.

June 1864	Congress grants equal pay to U.S. Coloured Troops.
June 1864	William Carney receives honourable discharge from the Union Army.
9th April 1863	General Lee surrenders at Appomattox, effectively ending the Civil War.
23rd May 1900	Carney receives the Medal of Honor.
9th December 1908	Carney dies after complications from a work-related accident.

HISTORICAL CONTEXT

SLAVERY

Beginning in 1619, white Europeans (and their descendants) living on the North American continent routinely kidnapped Black people from the African continent against their will and brought them across the ocean where they were treated like livestock and forced to work for no wages. These dehumanizing practices persisted for the next two centuries. In 1863, President Abraham Lincoln signed the Emancipation Proclamation which freed all enslaved people in the United States, but the Civil War was still underway, so many did not see freedom for several more years.

NEW BEDFORD, MASSACHUSETTS

This port city was home to a thriving whaling industry in the mid-1800s, as well as being known as a hub for abolitionist activity. New Bedford was an important stop on the Underground Railroad as well as a diverse destination city for many people escaping slavery.

ABOLITIONISTS

People who opposed slavery, which included free Black people and white people alike, predominantly in the northern United States. Many spoke out strongly against the human rights abuses and sought to see slavery outlawed. Some developed networks, known as the Underground Railroad, to help enslaved people escape to freedom.

JOHN BROWN

A noted white abolitionist, who believed that violence would ultimately be necessary to overturn the wrongs of slavery. In 1859, Brown led twenty-one men in a raid on the federal arsenal in Harpers Ferry, Virginia, hoping to capture weapons that could be used to arm enslaved people. The raid failed spectacularly, and Brown and several of his collaborators were caught, tried, convicted of treason and hanged.

FREDERICK DOUGLASS

He became a prominent abolitionist after escaping slavery himself. Douglass was a famous writer and orator whose words swayed many to the cause, including future president Abraham Lincoln. His strident advocacy for men of colour to enlist helped build the ranks of the 54th regiment.

THE CIVIL WAR

The issue of slavery vs abolition had divided the United States for decades and in 1861, the disagreement escalated to an armed conflict. A group of Southern states – who were committed to maintaining slavery as an institution – seceded from the Union with the goal of forming their own nation, the Confederate States of America. President Abraham Lincoln, an abolitionist, sought to preserve the nation as a whole and free its enslaved people.

54TH MASSACHUSETTS REGIMENT VOLUNTEERS

Massachusetts was among the first states to raise a Black regiment to fight in the Civil War. Men came from surrounding states to serve, and ultimately the unit comprised about one thousand men. Leaders of the Union Army hesitated to put the unit into service, as they worried that Black soldiers would not perform well, but the 54th showed exceptional courage during the assault on Fort Wagner and thereby changed hearts and minds within the army and around the country.

STARS AND STRIPES

A nickname for the flag of the United States of America. The flag has thirteen red and white stripes, representing the thirteen original colonies that formed the nation. The top left corner is a blue rectangle with a field of white stars representing the current states of the Union. Today, the flag bears fifty stars; the flag William Carney carried had thirty-four.

MINIÉ BALL/MINNIE BALL

The bullets used in Civil War-era rifles were conical, with a pointed tip and a flat base with oiled grooves around the outside. They were considered a technological improvement over the round musket balls used in previous wars, due to the ease of loading them into a long gun. They were also more damaging and deadly to the human body, due to their pointed shape.

PICKETS/PICKET LINE

In Civil War terminology, pickets were sentries who stood guard around a stationary campsite. They formed the first line of defence against enemy intruders – shots fired from the picket line alerted everyone in camp that a threat was approaching. When the unit was on the move, the term skirmish line or skirmishers was often used to describe a similar role, the men walking slightly ahead and outside of the lines, and the first to be engaged.

FORT WAGNER

Built by the Confederates in 1862 to defend Charleston Harbour, the fort is now most famous for being the site of the 54th regiment's courageous stand. Union forces finally succeeded in capturing the fort in 1863.

MARTHA BUSH GRAY

A Black nurse from New Bedford who served the 54th Massachusetts regiment after her husband and numerous friends had enlisted. William's interaction with her in the final chapter is entirely fictional, as she did not begin her service until 1864, but her story is important and fascinating. Martha bravely wrote to her congressman to gain permission to travel south and treat the Black soldiers, when few were willing to do so. She became known as the Mother of the 54th.

MEDAL OF HONOR

The United States' highest personal military decoration, presented to individuals who distinguish themselves through acts of extraordinary valour. Approximately 3,500 Medals of Honor have been presented in the award's history, with over forty per cent given for service during the Civil War.

JOHANNESBURG. MARCH 1961.

Thirty-one activists are on trial for treason. Among their numbers is Nelson Mandela, a rising star of the resistance movement and one of the biggest threats to the South African government and their racist system of apartheid. Along with the other activists, he is found not guilty. But rather than relish his newfound freedom, Nelson disappears. For months, he was an outlaw, hunted in vain by the police and the secret services, living under new identities and in various disguises, separated from his young family. His mission? To set up armed resistance to apartheid.